SOME COMME
COOL IS

Very useful. COOL IS BEST (CIB) shows us how to manage our emotions and how to share the Six Skills with others. It's fantastic!
A parent

The Six Skills help you to reflect and respond productively to situations as they arise.
A teacher

It was fun and I really liked the games!
A child, 8 years old

This has been extremely beneficial because many parents, teachers and children have learned how to be in control of their emotions.
A school psychologist

These are the kinds of educational and psychological workshops that our children need. Thank you!
A parent

We have seen a notable improvement in the self-regulation of the students and in the dynamic of the class.

A school director

I will pass on what I've learned to my children and students and I really believe that we can create change.

A teacher

If students learn to practice the 6 skills, conflicts in school would be quickly resolved.

A parent

CIB is important because it enables us to have more caring relationships.

A student, 17 years old

I learned that I can express my feelings and nothing bad happens.

A child, 10 years old

THE COOL IS BEST METHOD®

MAXIMUM WELL-BEING
for Parents, Teachers and Children

And How to Prevent Family Estrangement

JULIAN LANGINGER

First published by Cool is Best Publishing, 2024

Design by David Provolo

For information about special discounts for bulk purchases please contact Cool Is Best at info@coolisbest.com

ISBN 978-1-916724-00-6

First Edition

FOR MY FAMILY

AND FAMILIES
ALL AROUND THE WORLD

ACKNOWLEDGMENTS

A big thank you to the Cool is Best team: Irene Sambola, Albert Tarrès, Patri Urieta, Teresa Pretel, Leire López, Andrea Rodríguez, Silvia Ferrer, Cynthia Rodríguez, Patty Jarquín, María José Carranza, Isa Hernández, Kimberly Flores, Guillermo Monzón, Manel Agustín, Laia Capdevila, Elizabeth Lundberg, Bonaria Staffetta, Eider Agustín, Olivia Langinger, Gina Mesón and Laura Pretel; to Ferran Salmurri, Alicia Aleix, Backer Ali and Constancio Enciso for their constant support; to Lanette Sweeney, Jennie Swanson, David Provolo, three great editors and designers, Cristina Bacardit for her invaluable contribution, and Leo Langinger for his original sound design for the apps; and above all to the thousands of children, students, teachers and parents who have participated in the Cool is Best workshops, thank you all for your hard work and enthusiasm that has made this book possible.

NOTE TO READERS

Nothing in this book should be seen as clinical or psychological advice or as a substitute for professional expertise or treatment by a qualified mental health provider.

The words "emotions" and "feelings" are used interchangeably throughout.

TABLE OF CONTENTS

INTRODUCTION

This book is based on the "Cool is Best" method (CIB), which I founded in 2014 to train teachers, students and parents in the six skills of emotional intelligence which are recognized by psychologists worldwide as key to mental health and a life that is happy, responsible, productive and fulfilled.

I founded CIB because these skills had transformed my life away from anger, anxiety, depression, insecurity and stress to a place of great well-being, and I wanted to share the skills as widely as possible.

Since then, the destructive role of social media and other global issues have exacerbated mental health problems worldwide with daily reports on how health systems are being overwhelmed.* The WHO reported in 2019 that nearly one billion people were living with a mental health disorder and, in 2020, that 50% of worldwide mental health disorders begin at 14 years of age or before. At the same time, Mental Health America reported that in 2019-2020 more than 50 million Americans experienced a mental illness and that over half did not receive treatment. In the U.K., according to The Guardian in June 2023, students can wait an entire academic year for help.

Meanwhile it had become clear from the experiences reported by the thousands of teachers and parents who had learned the 6 Skills with COOL IS BEST and had gone on in 2021-2023 to train more than one hundred thousand children and students from 8 to 18 years (with some

* The crisis is much vaster than we realize. Washington Post 05.12.2022.

kindergarten teachers successfully adapting the program to children ages 4 and 5), that most people who learn to practice the Six Skills quickly feel better about themselves, are more accepting towards others and better able to create good relationships. Teaching adults and children on a large scale to practice the Six Skills would therefore seem to be an easily implementable, low-cost and preventive solution to a significant part of the global mental health crisis. At the same time, it would be an effective solution to bullying, another problem of epic proportions, because children and adults who practice empathy feel good about themselves and do not pick on others; and because children who practice the Six Skills have effective tools with which to stand up for themselves.

The Cool is Best team of psychologists began to teach the Six Skills in primary and secondary schools in Barcelona, Spain, in 2015 in a series of six or twelve 40-minute workshops. The results were extremely positive, with both teachers and parents commenting on notable improvements in well-being and behavior at home and in school.

Later that year, the Cool is Best team was invited by the director of a secondary school in one of the poorest districts of the city to do the workshops with a class of 12-to-13-year-olds, all recent immigrants from different countries and with very different backgrounds. The students were disruptive and uncooperative and, consequently, unable to concentrate and learn. After 12 workshops over a period of three months, the students participated in an outdoor event, during which they worked together in groups of four or five to complete a circuit of activities based on the Six Skills. A video of the event shows them relaxed and happy, working together in a way that would have been impossible just a few weeks earlier. I knew then that the Cool is Best method worked. It was fun and easy to teach and it produced good results in a remarkably short time.

At the same time, I had been traveling in Central America and was aware of the high student dropout rate there and the urgent need for a preventive educational program to address gender and gang violence. I thought the Cool is Best method could be of considerable help, but to be effective it had to reach large numbers of participants without the need for in-person workshops carried out by our team. I knew that many people had smart phones, and so I created the Cool is Best app for teachers, parents and children (see details at end of book). It contains the entire program in English and Spanish and includes videos of workshops, audios and interactive e-books. The app was adopted by a number of Ministries of Education in Latin America as part of their official social-emotional learning programs. It produces real-time reports that confirm that large numbers of teachers, parents and children have been trained in those countries with significant success.

Hundreds of videos went into the making of the app — of workshops with primary and secondary age children, and also of parent and seniors' workshops and teacher-training sessions. Almost all the participants commented positively on the benefits they gained from the course. But, to my surprise, the workshops were producing other unexpectedly positive results. Students talked about their feelings openly, many for the first time, and were receptive to and supportive of the feelings of their classmates. They talked about getting along better with their brothers and sisters at home and shared stories, often humorous, about learning to tolerate the more irritating qualities of their siblings. Many said that the experience of feeling calm in the mindful breathing moments was their favorite part of the workshops. Clearly there was a profound change in how the students related to others and how they felt about themselves. Teachers and parents also reported feeling more in control of their emotions and said that this made them better teachers and parents.

> "I have an annoying brother who has the ability to always get what he wants and, with COOL thinking (Skill 1) and conscious breathing (Skill 6), I can control how I feel."
>
> **Boy, 13 years old**
>
> *From video at the end of Cool is Best workshops*

I was also becoming more aware of what I now know to be a very common and widespread problem — family estrangement. Family estrangement is a painful, often heartbreaking, experience in which one member of a family cuts off contact and stops communicating with one or more of the other members, leaving those estranged in a never-ending limbo. Many of those who do the cutting off also suffer from regrets as well as remorse.

Estrangement impacts millions of people around the world. In the U.S. today over 100 million people (both estranged and estranging) are impacted, with all social classes, genders, and races being affected more or less equally; while in the U.K., the figure is 12 million.

Among my friends and colleagues, everyone knew someone who was affected by estrangement and many were baffled by the causes.

- "My friend Sarah's son doesn't allow her to visit her grandchildren, yet she remembers her son as a happy and loving child."
- "Bob hasn't spoken to his brother since their mother died. He's full of resentment and bitterness, and no one can understand it."
- "My daughter married a man who wrongly thinks that we don't like him. She never visits anymore."
- "My parents disapprove of my lifestyle and have told me I'm no longer welcome at home."

However, taking into account the work of Cool is Best over the previous seven or eight years, it seemed to me that parents would benefit from learning to practice the social and emotional skills necessary to create healthy relationships in their families in the first place, and to repair relationships if estrangement does take place, even where addiction is involved.*

I knew that our teachers, parents and students of all ages had acquired these very skills (rational thinking, healthy self-esteem, listening with empathy, communicating assertively while at the same time taking into account the desires of others, and having greater self-awareness), along with an ability to resolve even difficult conflicts on a win-win basis

---

* See References for books by Stanton Peele.

in a way that was satisfactory to all involved.

It is never too late to start practicing the Six Skills. In some circumstances, for example where the children are older, it may be helpful for parents to work with a counselor in order to learn how to regulate their emotions and listen to, and communicate with, their children more effectively.

In the case of estranged older children who have themselves become parents, they may change their attitudes and see their complaints in a different light if they learn to practice the Six Skills. One way for them to do this could be by doing the activities at the end of each chapter of this book, or on the app, together with their children.

Children who learn to practice the Six Skills — children who can talk about their feelings, manage their emotions and who have learned to listen with empathy, and who know how to resolve problems on a win-win basis — are likely to become adults who are less prone to grudges and feelings of resentment. They are less likely to become angry or withdrawn when things don't go their way, unlike children who are unable to manage their emotions and who therefore have very few tools available for navigating difficult situations when conflict occurs.

Factors in emotional well-being not related to the Six Skills

While this is beyond the scope of this book, it is important to know that emotional well-being can often be greatly improved by identifying and taking into account factors such as diet, food intolerances, exposure to harmful chemicals, exercise and physical health, as well as the effects of unresolved childhood trauma.

In this book

In this book you will learn how to practice the Six Skills that will enable you to overcome excessive anger, resentment, anxiety and depression, and have excellent mental health and happiness. At the same time the skills will help you to prevent estrangement, and to be at peace if estrangement should occur. Practicing the Six Skills will help you to look at your situation with different eyes and live more consciously, instead of ruminating over what went wrong. The skills will help you recognize that you are worthy of a happy, productive life even if things do not go the way you would like.

A SUMMARY OF THE SIX SKILLS

Skill 1: Managing our emotions

One of the main causes of anxiety, depression, excessive anger and estrangement is faulty thinking, also known as "HOT" thinking. HOT thinking is based on opinions, judgments and prejudices rather than on facts. When something happens that we don't like and our thinking is HOT, we may feel more upset than is warranted and consequently be more likely to reject others. The chapter on this skill shows you how you can learn to think in a helpful, "COOL" way that is based on facts rather than opinions, judgments and prejudices. COOL thinking enables us to feel good about ourselves and others, even when situations are not as we wish them to be.

The basis for this skill comes from Albert Ellis' REBT (Rational Emotive Behavioral Therapy) and the similar CBT (Cognitive Behavioral Therapy), but practiced preventively.

Skill 2: Recognizing and expressing our emotions

Studies show that being able to recognize our emotions and talk about how we feel when things happen that we don't like has the effect of helping us to feel less upset and behave better. Moreover, when we talk about how we feel, others are better able to understand our point of view about events and take this into account when problems arise.

Skill 3: Having healthy self-esteem

There is a common misconception that possessions, friends and accomplishments are what give us healthy self-esteem. This chapter shows that self-esteem is not based on external factors, but instead comes from thinking COOL thoughts (Skill 1) about oneself, such as "I accept myself just as I am" and "I will always value myself rather than put myself down." Contrary to popular belief, what we think of ourselves is far more important than what others think of us.

Skill 4: Listening with empathy

When someone has a problem, it is essential to listen to them with empathy so that they feel heard and valued. If we learn how to do this, other people will have warmer feelings towards us than they would otherwise have, we will have better relationships with them and problems will be more easily resolved.

Skill 5: Communicating with assertiveness

The way we communicate is of enormous importance in our relationships. When we communicate assertively, we take into account not only our own feelings and desires, but also those of other people. This is very different from communication that is aggressive or passive, and it is essential for being able to resolve problems and conflicts in a way that satisfies everyone involved.

Skill 6: Living consciously

Most of us go about our daily lives largely on automatic pilot, unaware of ourselves and of what goes on around us. When we live like this our unconscious mental chatter, which is often negative, influences or controls our decisions and causes us to suffer and even to see others as enemies. When we live consciously, we become more aware of ourselves and others and everything around us, and we see things as they really are rather than through a filter of judgments and prejudices. We feel more balanced, more at peace, and we are better able to have good relationships.

Engaging activities to do with your family

At the end of each chapter, you will find engaging and interesting activities to do with your family that will give you practice in the Six Skills.

> "Tell me and I forget, teach me and
> I may remember, involve me and I learn."
>
> **Benjamin Franklin**

Estrangement: the causes

The principal causes of estrangement:

1. Taking offense and perceiving slights where none were intended and not communicating effectively at the time.
2. Collecting grudges, ruminating on them, becoming increasingly resentful and bitter over time, and demonizing the "other."
3. Demanding that one's own wishes be met and being angry when others do not fulfill one's expectations.
4. Black-and-white thinking: there is no middle ground, it has to be my way.
5. Criticizing and blaming others and seeing oneself as a victim.
6. Jumping to erroneous conclusions that are not supported by facts.
7. Thinking that one's opinions and judgments are facts.
8. Thinking oneself superior to other people.
9. Demanding an apology for perceived wrongs, slights or transgressions that are not supported by the facts.
10. Being critical of the choices that others make.
11. Alienating a partner, or former partner, from their children.
12. Not accepting the marriages and divorces of others.
13. Being intolerant of values and lifestyles different from one's own.
14. Repeating family patterns by cutting people off in the same way others were previously cut off.
15. Having a faulty memory but insisting that it is reliable.

16. Having a lack of boundaries and being insensitive or abusive.
17. Parents favoring one child over another.
18. Feeling entitled.
19. Having disagreements over money; for example, concerning inheritances.
20. Making false accusations.
21. Being manipulated to cut off contact; for example, by a partner or a cult.
22. Projecting. Criticizing others for the very things one does, or has done, oneself in order to shift the focus from oneself onto the other person.
23. Having a lack of awareness of how others feel.

These causes are referred to below together with their respective numbers from 1 to 23.

Examples of family estrangement

In the following examples, you will see how estrangement could have been avoided if those involved had known about and practiced the Six Skills. All names are pseudonyms.

Example 1: Two sisters fall out over a disagreement

Jill and Paula are sisters who have always had an easygoing relationship. One day, after a disagreement between Jill and Paula's partner, Jill decided it would be better to not invite Paula and her partner to family events as it would be awkward. Paula was hurt and decided to have nothing more to do with her sister.

The principal cause of estrangement was:
Taking offense (1).

If Jill and Paula had known about and practiced the Six Skills, estrangement could have been avoided:
They would have been able to say to themselves, "I don't like what happened, but it's not the end of the world." (Skill 1). They would have listened to each other in order to understand how the other felt (Skills 2 and 4) and they would have considered each other's feelings and points of view and found a solution agreeable to both of them (Skill 5).

Example 2: Luke won't forgive his mother

Sandra's children all agree that she was interfering and bossy when they were growing up, but only Luke was filled with bitterness and resentment, cutting off all contact with his mother as soon as he was old enough to leave home. Many years later, and now with a family of his own, he refuses to see his mother, although his wife has arranged for their children to see their grandmother when he is not around.

The principal causes of estrangement were:
Lack of appropriate boundaries, and being insensitive or abusive (16)
Lack of awareness of how others feel (23)
Black-and-white thinking: it has to be my way (4)

If Sandra and Luke had known about and practiced the Six Skills, estrangement could have been avoided:
Sandra would have been aware (Skill 6) that her children

were not happy and would have listened to them (Skill 4) and changed her attitude (Skill 2). If she had found this difficult to do, she would have been aware enough to know that she should get the help of a counselor.

Later, when he was an adult, Luke would have understood that his mother had had a problem while he was growing up (Skill 4) and that there were alternatives to cutting her off, such as working on finding a solution that worked for both of them (Skills 1 and 5).

Example 3: A sister's lifetime's disapproval of her brother

To Bob's great dismay, shortly after their mother died, his sister Lucy came out with a long list of angry and bitter complaints about him, dating back to their early childhood. She told him she disapproved of his way of life, and accused him of not visiting her over the years and of not caring about her or her family. Although her accusations were demonstrably untrue, and she herself had not visited or shown interest in her brother's family, she demanded an apology for all his transgressions. When Bob tried to make amends by sending a note apologizing for not taking her feelings sufficiently into account, Lucy rejected his efforts as being wholly inadequate and cut off contact.

The principal causes of estrangement were:
Taking offense (1)
Collecting grudges (2)
Demandingness and angry rumination leading to bitterness when expectations are not met (3)
Blaming others and seeing oneself as a victim (5)

Thinking that one's opinions and judgments are facts (7)
Insisting that one's faulty memory is reliable (15)
Projecting (22)
Having a lack of awareness of how others feel (23)

If Lucy and Bob had known about and practiced the Six Skills, estrangement could have been avoided:
Lucy would have expressed her feelings about the events she was upset about at the time they occurred (Skill 2) instead of leaving them to grow and fester, and Bob would have therefore had the opportunity of taking his sister's feelings into account. Lucy would have been tolerant toward Bob's way of doing things (Skill 3) and she would have understood that it was not appropriate for her to make unpleasant comments about Bob (Skill 4). She would have communicated with assertiveness instead of aggressiveness and considered Bob's feelings and point of view as well as her own (Skill 5), instead of making demands based solely on what she herself wanted.

Moreover, she would have approached the situation in a way that enabled them to talk reasonably and resolve the problem (Skill 1) instead of making discussion impossible. She would have been aware enough to put aside any automatic negative thoughts she may have had (Skill 6). Bob would have been more aware of his sister's feelings about him (Skill 6) and been able to take them into account earlier.

Example 4: Tony's parents do not accept his partner

Tony's decision to marry against his parents' wishes has led to their complete estrangement from him, and caused problems for the members of the wider family as they continue to be in close contact with his siblings and cousins.

The principal causes of the estrangement were:
Demandingness: you must do as I say, or I will reject you (3)
Not accepting the marriages and divorces of others (12)
Intolerance of differences (13)

If Tony and his parents had known about and practiced the Six Skills, estrangement could have been avoided:
Tony's parents would have acted with tolerance and empathy (Skills 3 and 4). They would have been more able to discuss things calmly as a family and therefore it is more likely that they would have found a solution which did not result in cutting off contact with their son (Skill 5).

Example 5: Clara's divorce is not accepted by her children

After their mother Clara's decision to divorce their father, Emily and Alex chose to cut off all contact with her as a means of punishment. They felt that severing ties would serve as just consequences for the pain she had caused them, and prove their loyalty to their father who saw himself as the victim of his wife's unreasonable behavior.

The principal causes of the estrangement were:
Demandingness (3)
Not accepting the divorces of others (12)

If Emily and Alex had known about and practiced the Six Skills, estrangement could have been avoided:
They would have acted with empathy (Skill 4) and although they disapproved of the divorce, they would have understood that it was unhelpful to take sides and cut off contact (Skill 1). They would have looked for a solution that worked for everybody (Skill 5).

Example 6: A boyfriend isolates his partner

David and his girlfriend, Janna, were a young couple who had not been together long before David began to complain that her parents did not approve of their relationship. Janna and her parents tried to reassure him that this was not the case but he continued to find fault and to feel rejected by them and demanded that Janna choose between him and her family. Not understanding that she was in a relationship with a manipulative and abusive narcissist, it was not long before Janna found herself cut off from her friends and family.

The principal causes of estrangement were:
Taking offense (1)
Demanding to be given an excessive amount of attention (3)
Jumping to erroneous conclusions (6)

If David and Janna had known about and practiced the Six Skills, estrangement could have been avoided:
David would have had healthy self-esteem (Skill 3) and would not have needed other people to shower him with attention. He would have been able to talk about how

he felt (Skill 2) and resolve the issue through reasonable discussion (Skill 5).

Meanwhile, Janna would have been more aware of her situation (Skill 6) and more willing to talk the problem through (Skills 1 and 2) instead of blindly following David.

All parties would have listened to each other with empathy (Skill 4) and come to an amicable settlement (Skill 5).

For more on David and Janna's story, see the Epilogue and the role the Six Skills played in its outcome.

Example 7: Richard's wife has estranged their children from her husband

Richard and Cheryl have two children, and when the children were little, Cheryl began to alienate them from their father. At the same time, Cheryl was making his friends feel unwelcome and he gradually lost touch with many of them. As it turned out, she was doing what her own mother had done before her. Richard did not insist on his and his children's rights and he has not seen them since they were 10 and 12 years old.

The principal causes of estrangement were:
Alienating one's partner and children (11)
Repeating a family pattern (14)

If Richard and Cheryl had known about and practiced the Six Skills, estrangement could have been avoided:
Cheryl would have learned to be more aware (Skill 6) and empathic (Skill 4) and would have avoided causing pain to her children and their father. She would have thought in

a way that allowed all those affected to find a satisfactory solution to the situation (Skills 1 and 5).

Richard would have expressed his feelings (Skill 2), had healthy self-esteem (Skill 3), been assertive rather than passive (Skill 5), and would have taken whatever steps were necessary to maintain his relationship with his children.

Example 8: A father does not accept his son's choices

John and his father, Robert, became distant over time due to their conflicting values and expectations. Robert, stern and uncompromising, wanted his son to follow in his footsteps and devote himself to a career in which John had no interest. Despite John's attempts at reconciliation, his father's unwavering disapproval of his choices regarding his career and lifestyle drove a wedge between them. John stayed in contact with his mother but his father refuses to see him, a situation that is painful for them all.

The principal causes of estrangement were:
Demandingness and angry rumination leading to bitterness when expectations are not met (3)
Being critical of choices others make (10)
Being intolerant of values and lifestyles different from one's own (8)

If John and Robert had known about and practiced the Six Skills, estrangement could have been avoided:
Robert would have been more tolerant of his son's decisions, and when disagreements arose between them it is more likely he would have been able to listen with empathy and have

been more accepting of John's decisions. They would have both been more able to discuss things calmly and to respect each other's feelings and opinions.

Example 9: Jason estranged from his parents after he fell into a cult

Steven and Julia's son Jason went off to university and fell into a cult that was preying on new students. Within a short time, he came to believe that he had to leave his past behind him in order to be fully accepted by the other cult members, and soon after that he donated all his money and possessions to the cult. From this point on, Steven and Julia found it impossible to contact their son. He had been cut off from them by the cult.

The principal cause of estrangement was:
Being manipulated by a cult (21)

Jason found himself in a situation that he was not prepared to deal with. Cults are extraordinarily clever at capturing recruits. At first, they shower them with attention and love. Then they cut them off from their contacts. Then they take their money. Then, when the recruits feel powerless and confused, they subjugate them.

It is essential that parents educate their children about the danger of cults and sects so that if they come into contact with one, they are able to recognize what is happening. If that should happen, they need to know above all that they must immediately remove themselves from the situation in order to avoid the real possibility that the cult captures them.

They need to know that being swallowed up can happen very quickly, within hours.

If Steven, Julia and their son Jason had known about and practiced the Six Skills, estrangement could have been avoided:

Although the subject of cults is beyond the scope of this book, the Six Skills foster open communication and encourage parents and children to express their thoughts and feelings, to listen with empathy and to be assertive — all essential skills when helping a family member avoid being recruited by a cult.

SKILL 1

MANAGING OUR EMOTIONS

Being Able to Make
Good Decisions

This chapter shows you how you can think in a way that helps you be in control of your emotions and therefore feel good, or less bad, in the circumstances in which you find yourself. This is called COOL thinking.

With COOL thinking, we base our thoughts on facts rather than judgments. We say things to ourselves such as, "I don't like what is happening, but it could be worse, and I can find a solution to it."

In contrast, with HOT thinking, we say things to ourselves such as, "What is happening is terrible and I can't stand it." HOT thinking is based on judgments, opinions and prejudices that cause us to have stronger unpleasant feelings than necessary when things happen that we don't like.

Having the habit of COOL thinking enables us to talk in a reasonable way about problems with others and find solutions to them. As a result, we avoid hostility and grudges from taking root and possibly causing estrangement later.

What causes us to feel and behave the way we do?

Many people believe that the way they feel and behave is determined by the events and experiences that happen in their lives. Saying things such as, "You made me angry" or "She pushed my buttons" shows that we assume our feelings and behaviors are caused by things that happen outside of ourselves. If we live our lives believing that to be true, we will be happy when things turn out the way we wish and unhappy when they do not. This means that we will be setting ourselves up to lose control of our emotions, because the way things turn out is often not within our control.

However, when we really think about it, we can see that events and experiences alone do not cause us to feel the way we do. Not everyone feels and behaves the same way when faced with the same event.

If, for example, we are traveling on a crowded train at rush hour and someone bumps into us roughly and we drop our belongings, we may be annoyed or even angry. But if we then see that the person who bumped into us is blind, our feelings change immediately. This shows that it is mainly the way we think about and interpret events, not the events themselves, that cause us to feel and behave the way we do.

Knowing that we can choose how we feel and act is the key to living a truly happy and productive life. We can choose how we think and, by doing so, determine how we feel and behave. And when we are in control of our emotions, we are more able to accomplish the goals we set for ourselves.

> "What upsets people is not things themselves but their judgments about things."
>
> **Epictetus**
>
> *Stoic philosopher living in Ancient Rome*

Major discoveries by two renowned scientists

In his book *The Biology of Belief*, Bruce Lipton recounts how he was living his life in a depressed and fatalistic way as a scientist at Stanford University, when he had a life-changing moment. He realized that the results of his research on cells proved that he had lived his academic life on the basis of an error. His scientific education had taught him that our genes control our lives, whereas he now saw that his research proved that it is our environment — including the way we think about things — that controls our genes. He realized in that moment that he could choose to think differently and direct his life, rather than be a passive bystander or a victim of it.

> "Changing the way we live and the way we perceive the world changes our biology."
>
> **Bruce Lipton**
>
> *The Biology of Belief*

Richard Davidson, a neuroscientist who studies emotions by scanning people's brains, confirms that his own research led him to arrive at the same conclusion:

> "The amazing fact is that through mental activity alone we can intentionally change our own brains."
>
> **Richard Davidson**
>
> *The Emotional Life of Your Brain*

"Intentional neuroplasticity" is the recently coined term for changing our brains intentionally, and Davidson reports that his research shows that we can change our brains quite quickly with practice.

Athletes are a good example of using intentional neuroplasticity: they talk to themselves positively and visualize winning their event in order to give themselves a better chance of winning. We, too, can repeat the thoughts that we want to arise automatically in our minds and create a new habit that helps us in our lives. You can practice doing this at the end of this chapter (see Activities).

A major discovery in psychology

Albert Ellis realized the critical importance of the way people think while working as a psychologist in New York in the 1950s. He came to see that the Freudian approach he was using, which was based on the idea that emotional disturbance and counterproductive behavior has its roots in childhood events and experiences, helped his patients to learn about their childhoods but did not help them overcome their emotional problems in the present.

Being familiar with the teachings of Buddha and the philosophers of ancient Greece and Rome, who thousands of years ago recognized that the way we think is the key to emotional peace and self-control, he asked himself if his patients were disturbed because of their thoughts in the present rather than because of past traumas they had endured.

In order to test his hypothesis, he asked his patients to do two things: first, identify the kind of unhelpful and irrational thoughts and beliefs (HOT thinking) that might be causing their emotional distress and counterproductive behavior and, second, change them for the kind of rational and helpful thinking (COOL thinking) that promotes healthy feelings, emotional well-being and appropriate, constructive behavior.

Ellis's hypothesis was borne out by results. The emotional health of the participants of the trial, who changed their thinking from HOT to COOL, improved significantly. Ellis went on to develop REBT (Rational Emotive Behavioral Therapy), which was followed later by the development of CBT (Cognitive Behavior Therapy) by another psychologist, Aaron Beck. These therapies that focused on changing a person's thoughts soon changed the way psychological counseling was practiced worldwide. Since then, large numbers of studies have confirmed the effectiveness of substituting HOT thinking with COOL thinking in helping both adults and children resolve emotional and behavioral problems. It is important to note that HOT and COOL in this context refer to thoughts. Emotions are not considered HOT or COOL, they are simply emotions that may be agreeable or disagreeable.

HOT thoughts cause us to feel worse than we need feel in any given situation. They are not based on facts but on judgments, assumptions and prejudices, and they cannot be shown by evidence to be true.

COOL thoughts are based on demonstrable facts and can be shown by evidence to be true. COOL thoughts cause us to feel better and to be resilient in the face of the obstacles and inevitable setbacks of life. Adults and children who think COOL are not so easily upset and are therefore able to think more clearly, make better decisions and persevere when faced with challenging situations. They are more in control of themselves and their lives, feel more relaxed and balanced, think more clearly, make better decisions,

---

NOTE: In the 1980s the American Psychological Association voted Albert Ellis the second-most important psychologist of the past 100 years after Carl Rogers (see Skill 4).

create better relationships and have significantly greater happiness and sense of well-being.

> "It's not what you look at that matters,
> it's what you see."
> **Henry David Thoreau**
> *Walden*

The goal of COOL thinking is not to suppress negative feelings but to enable us to think with rational and helpful thoughts that result in feelings and behaviors that are healthy and appropriate. When we think COOL, unpleasant feelings do not necessarily disappear — we may still feel disappointed if, for example, we do badly, but we do not feel a total failure, as we might if we thought HOT. Our feelings are healthy and we acknowledge them and are then able to move on. When we think rationally and helpfully, our feelings do not fluctuate wildly; we keep calm and think clearly even in difficult situations, such as when someone criticizes us unjustly. We can learn to think COOL and to convert our HOT thoughts to COOL. Adults will need commitment and persistence to modify their HOT thoughts because they tend to have established patterns of thoughts, beliefs, and judgments, whereas children can modify their HOT thoughts more easily because they do not yet have such deeply rooted habits.

An example of converting HOT thinking to COOL thinking:

Situation: I have lost my phone — with HOT thinking

Here is the same situation, but with COOL thinking

Choosing to think COOL thoughts is an extremely powerful way to improve one's life. In his book *The Emotional Life of the Brain*, Richard Davidson confirms that studies show that "cognitive reappraisal," the process of choosing effective new ways to think, "can significantly improve well-being among those suffering from depression."

In *A Guide to Personal Happiness*, Albert Ellis emphasized that, while thinking COOL rather than HOT is extremely effective in helping us overcome existing emotional and behavioral problems, it is even more important to use it preventively to avoid having problems in the first place.

Learning to practice COOL thinking is one of the most important things we can do to prevent estrangement.

> "It is more difficult to crack a prejudice than to split an atom."
>
> **Albert Einstein**

A summary of Ellis's ABC model

A - An activating event or experience — something happens.

B - Beliefs and thoughts — our beliefs and thoughts about A.

C - Consequences, emotional and behavioral — the way we feel and behave.

If we have uncomfortable or distressed feelings or behave in a counterproductive way, and if we want to feel less disturbed and behave more constructively, we continue to D.

D Dispute — we dispute/challenge our beliefs and thoughts (B) to see whether they are COOL, that is, that they are both (i) true and (ii) helpful to us. If they are either not true or not helpful (i.e., they are HOT), we continue to E.

E - Effective new COOL thoughts — we find thoughts that help us feel better and behave in more appropriate ways.

The ABCs: Changing thoughts from HOT to COOL — with examples

NOTE: One's way of thinking can be entrenched, and it is therefore important to do the ABCs with conviction, commitment, determination and persistence in order to satisfy ourselves that our HOT thoughts do not stand up to scrutiny. With practice, we can become able to calm our aroused feelings in an instant.

A – Activating event

Think of a disagreeable event or experience and your feelings about it. Describe what happened — just the facts, without any comment or judgment. For example, "Someone criticized me."

____

____

____

____

____

____

B – Beliefs and thoughts

Write down what you thought/said to yourself regarding A. For example, "Nobody should criticize me."

____

____

____

____

____

____

C – Consequences (the feelings that follow)

Identify and write down your main feeling (it could be angry, anxious, depressed, etc.). For example, "I felt angry."

Note how strong your feeling was on a scale of 1 to 10. For example, "8" (very angry).

Describe your behavior after the event. For example, "I avoided them."

D – Dispute/challenge my thoughts

If you want to change the way you feel, dispute/challenge your beliefs and thoughts. Really question whether your thought is justified by the facts and whether it helps you feel good about things in the circumstances.

For example, "My thought is not based on fact — there is no evidence that people *should not* criticize me simply because I wish it to be so."

"My thought is not helpful to me. I would feel less angry if I did not *demand* that people *should not* criticize me unfairly."

Is my thought HOT or COOL? For example, "It is HOT."

E – Effective new thoughts (COOL thoughts)
Once we are sure that our thought is HOT, we look for effective new beliefs and thoughts (i.e., COOL thoughts) that will enable us to feel the way we want to feel and achieve our goals more easily.

We ask ourselves: What can we think that will help us reduce our feelings of upset and feel better in these circumstances?

We write the thoughts down and choose the one that really works for us. For example, "I don't like it if someone criticizes me, but it is not the end of the world if they do. I can bear it and I might even learn something from it!"

____

____

____

____

Once we have a new COOL thought we can try it out by thinking it consciously and asking ourselves how we feel now, and at what intensity, and we compare this to how we felt before. And we see that thinking with COOL thoughts reduces the intensity of our disagreeable emotions.

For example, "I felt angry but now I just feel annoyed."

"I felt anxious but now I just feel concerned."

"I felt depressed but now I just feel sad."

COOL thoughts can also lead to a complete change of emotion. For example, "I felt angry but now what happened doesn't affect me at all."

"I felt anxious but now I feel relaxed."

"I felt depressed but now I feel happy."

If this happens, write down some comments about the change in your feelings.

Now write down your change in behavior as a result of the way you are now feeling. For example, "I am no longer avoiding the person who criticized me. I talked to them in order to resolve the issue."

Short ABC Form — with example

SHORT ABC FORM	
A-What happened? Just the facts	"They criticized me."
B-What did I think/say to myself?	"Everyone should always be nice to me and certainly not criticize me."
C-How did I feel and behave? **Intensity out of 10**	"I felt angry, and I avoided them." 8
D-Was my thought based on facts? **Did it help me feel good?** **Was it HOT or COOL?**	"My thought was not based on facts — there is no evidence that people *should not* criticize me simply because I wish it to be so." "My thought did not help me feel good. I would feel less angry if I did not *demand* that people *should not* criticize me." My thought was HOT.

E-My new COOL thought	"I don't like it if someone criticizes me, but it is not the end of the world if they do. I can bear it and I might learn something from it!"
How do I feel now?	"I feel annoyed but not angry."
Intensity out of 10	2 instead of 8
My behavior	"I am no longer avoiding the person who criticized me unfairly. I talked to them in order to resolve the issue."

Short ABC Form — blank

SHORT ABC FORM	
A-What happened? Just the facts	
B-What did I think/say to myself?	
C-How did I feel and behave? **Intensity out of 10**	

D-Was my thought based on facts? **Did it help me feel good?** **Was it HOT or COOL?**	
E-My new COOL thought **How do I feel now?** **Intensity out of 10** **My behavior**	

HOT and COOL thoughts contrasted

HOT thoughts and beliefs cause us to have unpleasant feelings:

- They are based on judgments, opinions, interpretations, suppositions, and demands, rather than on facts that are verifiable.
- They are unhelpful — we (and others) feel worse because of them.
- They are based on one or more of the many common HOT ways to think (see later).

COOL thoughts and beliefs make us feel good, or better:

- They are based on facts that can be verified.

- They are helpful to us — they lead to outcomes we desire such as feeling good.
- They are based on moderate rather than extreme and exaggerated thinking.

"I have learned that for every HOT thought there is a COOL thought."
A parent
From video at the end of Cool is Best workshops

What it means if we think that our feelings and behavior are determined by events or other people's actions

1. Our feelings are largely at the mercy of events and what other people do or don't do, and, as we often do not have control over events, this means that we do not have control over our feelings. If we do not have control over our feelings, which play such a big part in our lives, this means that we do not have control over our lives.
2. As a consequence, we may develop the habit of either suppressing our feelings or reacting strongly and acting them out.
3. We become dependent on events turning out the way we want in order for us to be happy.
4. We may spend a large amount of time and energy futilely trying to change things when we think we have, or may have, the power to do so.
5. We may have a tendency to not take responsibility for our feelings and behavior, to blame events and

other people for the way we feel and behave, and to think of ourselves as victims.

6. We may escape into harmful pursuits such as drinking, using drugs, smoking, overeating, avoidance, or opting out, in order to assuage our distressed feelings of anxiety, anger, or depression, and of not being in control of our lives and not being able to cope.

Children and adults who see other family members as the causes of their misfortunes may build up an accumulation of grudges and use these as the basis for rejection and estrangement in later years. This can happen at any time; for example, upon the death of a parent, when the estranging person may feel there is no longer anything to hold them back.

What it means if we understand that our feelings and behavior are largely caused by the way we think

1. We choose the way we think and regulate the way we feel even if events and other people's actions are not ideal.
2. Suppressing our feelings, which is counterproductive, doesn't arise because we can choose the way we think and therefore choose the way we feel.
3. We can think in a way that is helpful to us about whatever happens, and therefore not be dependent on things turning out the way we want in order to be happy.
4. We do not need to try to change other people and, as a result, we can have better relationships with them and save ourselves a large amount of time and energy trying to change them.

5. We do not blame other people or events but rather take responsibility for our feelings and behavior and do not think of ourselves as victims.
6. We are in control of ourselves and feel relaxed and satisfied and have no need to escape into risky or harmful behaviors.

Family members who have learned to think COOL will have goodwill and base their thinking on facts. They will avoid exaggeration and demandingness, and it is extremely unlikely that they will estrange from other family members in later years.

Choosing COOL thoughts in line with our values

COOL thoughts and beliefs are helpful, but we also want them to be in line with our values. There is no place for adopting new thoughts and beliefs that do not respect other people, their rights and their freedoms.

> "Self-control and self-confidence
> will lead to great vices if they are
> not paired with humility and gentleness."
>
> **Rudolf Steiner**
>
> *The Inner Development of Man*

Therefore, while we can choose to think in such a way that enables us to feel happier, more confident, stronger, less dependent, less disturbed and so on, we can also listen to our conscience and choose to be humble, caring, kind, tolerant, compassionate and generous in order to ensure that we do not become intolerant, hurtful or selfish.

Self-talk

It may seem surprising but all of us — adults and children alike — talk to ourselves much of the time. This self-talk arises in our minds automatically and we are usually not aware of it, or only barely aware of it. It can be full of judgments and opinions and it can be extremely critical, both of ourselves and of others. We repeat these HOT thoughts to ourselves again and again and gradually come to believe them until they become established patterns of thinking that determine how we feel and behave. Because we are so familiar with this "script," it seems to be based on "facts" rather than opinions. It makes sense to us, and we come to feel comfortable with it.

It is as if at an extremely early age, we write a script and then live our lives according to it. It is like a tape in our head that plays spontaneously and, because we are not aware of it, we cannot turn it off.

Albert Ellis pointed out that we indoctrinate ourselves by thinking and talking to ourselves in this way so that, for example, if we make a mistake, we may tell ourselves repeatedly, "I can never ever do anything right!" and then think that we are stupid or useless.

Or we may have a similar thought about somebody else who could be a brother or sister or parent or acquaintance and then think that they are stupid or useless or that they have behaved towards us in unacceptable ways that later lead us to say to ourselves, "Those remarks that my sister made years ago are unacceptable and so I no longer want to have anything more to do with her."

Throughout our lives, we adopt the thoughts and beliefs that make up our self-talk from sources around us — ourselves, our family, our teachers, our friends, people we meet, and from literature, TV, film and the media, thoughts such as, "I'm no good unless I'm the best" or "Other people must like me or I'm no good" or "You're nobody 'till somebody loves you," the words of a popular song.

These kinds of thoughts often cause us to have uncomfortable or distressed feelings about ourselves and other people and to behave in ways that are not in our best interests. Moreover, an unpleasant feeling caused by one of these thoughts can lead to more unhelpful self-talk, which is then followed by more distressed feelings. For example, if, in response to some event, I think, "I am a failure," I may feel anxious or depressed and as a result I may withdraw. This can then lead me to have the further thought, "See, I am doing nothing. I was right, I am a failure," which leads to further unhealthy feelings, and so on.

We can have extraordinarily long memories. In *Vanity Fair*, William Thackeray writes of the old man who trembles when he remembers the beating his schoolmaster gave him when he was a child.

Being beaten would be a very painful and humiliating experience. But think also of the adult sibling who feels bitter and resentful over a small thing that occurred with a brother or sister when young, and who dwells on it and nurtures it over the years into a self-blinding hate, often reinforced by those around them who only know one side of the story. How many relationships and lives have been blighted by the inability to put events in a realistic and manageable perspective because of obsessive HOT thinking?

Jon Kabat Zinn, creator of MBSR (Mindfulness-Based Stress Reduction), who has worked with and helped people recover from depression for many years, has reported that all participants in the program had the same self-defeating thoughts yet believed that they were alone in having them.

For this reason, it is important to talk with your children about your and their thoughts and feelings. Talking about our thoughts and feelings in a supportive environment (Skill 4, listening with empathy) helps everyone to know that they are not alone and to put their thoughts and feelings in perspective.

Self-talk and automatic negative thoughts (ANTs)

Both Albert Ellis and Aaron Beck, the creator of Cognitive Behavior Therapy, identified the counterproductive thoughts and beliefs that act as a filter through which we see and respond to life. Aaron Beck called a number of them Automatic Negative Thoughts (ANTs).

ANTs have the following characteristics:

- They are all examples of HOT thinking.
- We are barely aware of them or not aware of them at all.
- We therefore don't question them.
- We repeat them to ourselves in our self-talk until we believe in them without question, even if they are false.

- We pick them up from a variety of sources — from our family, from our surroundings and from all the people we are in contact with as we grow up.
- They often cause us to have strong disagreeable feelings.

Because of the unhelpful things that we say to ourselves, it is more difficult for us to attain our goals. For example, if we think, without being aware of it, "I'm not capable of doing this," we create a self-fulfilling prophecy and will find it more difficult to do what we are trying to do.

When we talk to ourselves with ANTs, we have uncomfortable or unpleasant feelings, and this discomfort then acts as a trigger for more ANTs.

Our ANTs can undermine our relationships with others, including family members, and lead to estrangement.

On the following pages, you will find the most common self-defeating thoughts and how to change some of them into more helpful thoughts.

COMMON HOT WAYS TO THINK THAT ARE OFTEN AUTOMATIC

1. Exaggerating thinking

An example of exaggerating thinking in response to making a mistake might be to think that it is "awful" or a "disaster." This kind of thinking makes us have stronger unpleasant feelings than needed and, because we feel bad, we are less likely to think rationally and are therefore less able to find the best solution for situations in which we find ourselves. Moreover, the feelings these thoughts provoke may then cause us to behave in ways that are not in our interests.

The best way to avoid exaggerating is to be aware that it is self-defeating and to be aware of when we do it. We ask ourselves, “Is what I am thinking true? Is it true that it’s a disaster?” and “Is my thought helpful to me, or harmful?” Then when we have the answers, we can choose to think without exaggeration.

A student running in a relay race drops the baton and thinks, “I dropped the baton and it’s a disaster.” He thinks that it is the worst thing that he could have done and feels deeply ashamed and humiliated. However, when he asks himself, “Is it true that it is a disaster?” he realizes that there are many worse things that can happen in life and that this kind of thinking makes him feel worse than necessary. He sees that we all make mistakes and that dropping the baton can happen to anyone, and he feels much better.

> **"When something happens between me and my brother, it (the Six Skills) helps me to keep calm and not argue."**
>
> **Boy, 9 years old**
>
> *From video at end of Cool is Best workshops*

When we exaggerate, we often do not consider all the factors involved. For example, your children may do poorly on an important exam and say to themselves, “My grades are not as good as they need to be, and I won’t get a place at the university I want to go to, and it’s awful, it’s terrible, it’s a disaster.” As a result, they may feel like failures despite their high level of achievement. Yet it might turn out that going to another university would be just as good a choice or an even better one!

It can be very helpful to also remember that something we think is terrible today may seem far less serious later.

2. Demanding thinking

Demandingness is one of the most common kinds of HOT thinking, and it can be very destructive. The words "must," "should," "ought to" and "have to" can, of course, be used in harmless ways that do not lead to strong emotional reactions such as, for example, when we say, "I must water the flowers."

However, demands we make in the sense of *absolutely must*, *absolutely should*, *absolutely ought to* and *absolutely have to* are harmful and self-defeating because, when things do not work out the way we demand, we may have feelings such as anger, anxiety or depression. And these kinds of feelings may then cause us to behave in self-defeating ways.

An extremely effective antidote to demandingness is to think instead with preferences, to say to oneself, "I *prefer* — or strongly prefer — but I do not *demand* it."

> "You can only be happy if you do not expect anything."
>
> **André Comte-Sponville**
> *Contemporary French philosopher*

Demands on ourselves

Some examples of demands we may make on ourselves:

"I *must* win the game."

"I *should never* make mistakes."

"I *ought to* have what I want."

"I *have to* get top marks in the exam."

If your children think, possibly without being fully aware of it, "I *must* get an A on the exam," this thinking may make them feel anxious and therefore less able to study calmly and obtain good results.

If they then do worse than they *demand*, they are likely to have stronger unpleasant feelings such as anger or depression than they would have had if they had thought in a nondemanding way with preferences, and furthermore, these feelings may cause them to act in counterproductive ways.

Meanwhile, if you as a parent make demands on yourself such as "I *must* be a perfect parent," you are likely to have strong uncomfortable feelings if you are not the perfect parent.

The solution is to think with preferences instead of demands:

For example, "I would *prefer* — or strongly prefer — to get top marks in the exam." Or "I would *prefer* — or strongly prefer — to be a perfect parent."

And "I will try my very best but if I do not succeed, that's OK because no one can be perfect. If I do my best, that is good enough. No one can do better than their best."

Demands on others

Being demanding towards others is also extremely harmful,

to ourselves and to our relationships. We would do far better to change ourselves than to try to change others.

Here are two examples:

Alex wanted his siblings to do things his way and, when they did not do so, he cut off from them.

Had he *preferred* — or even strongly preferred — rather than *demanded* that his siblings did things his way, he would have had less strong feelings and would have been less likely to cut off from them.

Marta believed that marriage should last forever, effectively a *demand* that nobody should ever divorce. So, when her mother decided to divorce, Marta estranged from her.

These kinds of estrangements would not happen if we thought COOL and recognized that everyone is free to make their own decisions about their lives.

> "My mother is the person who I get angry with most. Now, instead of getting angry, I can control myself better."
>
> **Girl, 13 years old**
>
> *From video at the end of a Cool is Best workshop*

3. Having low frustration tolerance (LFT)

Thinking with LFT is common, and it arises from *demandingness* and *exaggeration*. We say to ourselves that something "*should* be easy," and when it isn't easy, we exaggerate, saying that "it's too difficult" and "it is unbearable" and "I can't stand it."

When we think like this, we feel more upset than we need to in the circumstances, and we may put off doing what we were going to do.

For example:

"I can't stand it when I have to mow the grass (an implicit demand that I should not have to mow the grass), I'll do it later."

"I have homework to do, but homework is boring, and I hate being bored. It's terrible to be bored, I can't stand it. I'm going to watch TV instead."

This kind of thinking makes us feel worse than we need to feel in the circumstances and causes procrastination, which itself is likely to lead to more counterproductive self-talk such as "I'm hopeless" or "I can't get things done" — which in turn leads to more uncomfortable feelings and lower self-esteem.

Furthermore, if we do not do the work that is required, we miss out on the satisfaction that comes from putting in the effort.

We can help ourselves and our children develop high frustration tolerance by helping them to see that frustration is an inevitable part of life. Over time we can come to realize that there is very little that we cannot stand if we have COOL helpful thoughts in our minds.

> "No one can prove that my life conditions have got to be hassle free and it is practically certain that they won't always be."
>
> **Albert Ellis**

4. Projecting

Projecting is unconsciously taking traits we don't like about ourselves or our behavior and attributing them to someone else, and criticizing them for having the same characteristics. It is an attempt to make ourselves feel better and superior. We criticize others rather than look at ourselves.

Projecting is very common among family members who estrange. For example, the sibling who has insulted and criticized and rejected another family member and does so on the grounds that that family member has not been friendly — when in fact it was the estranging family member who has been unfriendly and who has driven away his siblings by his unpleasantness, insults, criticisms and accusations that had no basis in fact.

5. Jumping to erroneous conclusions

We jump to an erroneous conclusion when we make an assumption that is not true and do not check the facts.

For example, "He doesn't care about me because he didn't call me," or "She must be angry with me because she didn't text me back."

In order to avoid jumping to erroneous conclusions it is important to make a special effort regarding emails, text messages and tweets, as they tend to be hastily written and open to different interpretations.

> "There are people who suffer from
> a wrong perception for 10 or 20 years.
> They are sure the other person has betrayed them or
> hates them, even though it is false,
> and the other person has good intentions."
>
> "It is helpful to write
> *'Are you sure you are right?'*
> on a piece of paper and
> put it up in your room."
>
> **Thich Nhat Hanh**

Walt estranged from his sister late in life. He said, "You never cared about me or my family." He had jumped to a false conclusion and would not accept that his sister did indeed care about him and his family.

6. Taking things personally and taking offense

It is very easy to take things personally and to take offense where none was intended. It is much harder not to do so. When we take things personally, we think that what people think or do is related to ourselves or directed against us, even though this is not necessarily the case. For example, someone may give us a funny look and we are sure they are making some adverse judgment about us.

Taking things personally often causes us to take offense, hold grudges and even cut off relations with someone who is, or has been, a close friend or family member. If we think COOL, however, we are aware of this danger and can avoid it by thinking, "Well, I could take offense or I could avoid taking offense, deal with the issue, and continue to have a good relationship with that person."

> "The Dalai Lama looks at
> his caricatures and smiles."
>
> **Thubten Wanchen**
>
> *Interview in "La Vanguardia" at the time of the Mahomet caricatures.*

7. Black-and-white thinking

This occurs when we think about things in all-or-nothing or either-or terms. We think that something is completely good or completely bad, that it is either a success or a failure. We think that someone is either bright and interesting or dull and boring, rather than someone with a combination of different qualities. In black-and-white thinking, there are no half tones and no middle ground.

Examples of this kind of thinking:

"Either you're for me or you're against me."
"You are awful, there is nothing good about you."

People who think like this can pass quickly from feeling supremely happy to feeling profoundly depressed. They fall out with people easily — all it takes is for someone to do something they consider to be unacceptable, even if it is objectively not that bad. One minute everything is rosy and the next minute everything is black.

People who estrange might think that members of their family have done things they don't like, and they reject them. They ignore all the positive things that those family members have done.

8. Magnifying the negative and minimizing the positive

Magnifying and minimizing arise when we think selectively: we magnify the negative and minimize the positive aspects of any situation.

For example, we magnify our defects and downplay our strong points, and we do the same thing regarding other people. If we come second in a race, we may think, "Only winning is any good" and ignore the fact that coming second can be a great achievement — and that, in any case, not everyone can win.

If we magnify and minimize, we may ignore things that are positive about ourselves and others, we are unnecessarily critical and never feel that things are good enough.

An estranging family member may think that their criticisms of other family members are what is important and that any transgressions of their own have no importance.

9. Mind-reading

Mind-reading occurs when we believe we are sure that we know what others are thinking about us or why they behave towards us the way they do.

For example, in response to seeing two people looking at us, we may think:

"I know they are saying bad things about me." But, of course, it is impossible to know what someone is thinking unless they tell you!

In this situation we can say to ourselves, "It doesn't matter to me what they think," and feel perfectly fine. Of course, for this thought to be effective, it is essential that we believe it.

Mind-reading can cause estrangement. For example, the brother who cut off from his sister and said, "I remember perfectly that 40 years ago you intended to cheat me," when he was in fact totally wrong about his accusation and couldn't possibly have read his sister's mind and known what she was thinking.

10. Generalizing

To generalize is to think that something that is true some of the time is true all of the time.

The words "always," "never," "everyone," "nobody," "every," and "none" are words to watch out for because they often indicate that we are generalizing — or that someone else is doing so. For example, a student who thinks "I did badly, and I'll *never* be any good at this"; such a generalization is self-defeating and may make it less likely that the student will take steps to do well.

An estranging adult sibling may say, "You never visited me" because that is what he tells himself and what he thinks he remembers, even though his sister had indeed visited on multiple occasions over the years.

> "Cool is Best helps me to see things in a different way."
>
> **Young person, 18 years old**
>
> *From questionnaire at the end of Cool is Best workshops*

11. Labeling

This occurs when we use a label to refer to someone. For example, we may say, "Jim is a trouble-maker" and thereafter only see the trouble Jim is causing rather than the positive things that he does. Meanwhile, Jim may also see himself as a troublemaker even if he is not, and ignore his own good points.

A label can become part of a person's identity and come to be seen as something that cannot be changed. A boy calls a teammate "useless" because he loses the ball during a game of football. Now he, and maybe others who heard the comment, think of the teammate as useless, even though he has many positive qualities.

When parents use labels, even those used with affection, there is the danger that a family member may remember the label and use it as a pretext to estrange from another family member, insisting that the term had been meant pejoratively and was a true description of the person, even many years later.

12. Emotional reasoning

This occurs when we confuse facts and feelings — we think that something must be so because we *feel* it to be so — even if there is no factual evidence that validates the feeling.

For example, we feel hurt and are convinced that a particular person has done something against us even if, in fact, they have not: "I feel that Dani ignored me and, therefore, he *must have* ignored me," or "I feel stupid and therefore I am stupid."

When we think about it, it becomes obvious that thinking in this way will create problems and that we will do well to notice so that we can put a stop to it.

13. Egocentric thinking

If we think egocentrically, we think that we are always right. We may also think that other people must have the same point of view and the same values that we have and, if they don't, they are wrong. We think that other people cannot and should not see things differently to the way we see things.

Thinking like this, not respecting the fact that others have a right to think differently, is disastrous for relationships. Family members who estrange may think like this, believing that they are right no matter what the other says and no matter what the evidence.

ACTIVITIES TO DO TOGETHER WITH YOUR CHILDREN

PARENT GUIDE: SKILL 1

MANAGING MY EMOTIONS

INTRODUCTION

These activities should be adapted to the ages of the children participating and to your own parental circumstances.

If you find the Six Skills helpful, you can download the app Cool is Best The 6 Skills, where you will find additional resources including videos, audios and interactive e-books for children from 8 to 14 years old.

Note for teachers: these activities are used successfully in Cool is Best workshops with students in school.

INDEX OF ACTIVITIES (40 MINS)

1. Objectives, usefulness, materials
2. Introduction (5 mins)
3. Activity (20 mins)
4. Reflections (5 mins)
5. What have we learned today? The usefulness of the skill (5 mins)
6. Conscious breathing (5 mins)
7. What to do between sessions
8. Materials for use during the activities

1a. OBJECTIVES

- Learning that there are two ways of thinking: HOT and COOL.
- Learning that thinking COOL helps me to feel better and thinking HOT makes me feel worse than necessary.
- Realizing that I can change my thoughts from HOT to COOL and feel good or not so bad.
- Understanding that HOT and COOL apply to thoughts, not to situations or emotions.
- Learning that a COOL thought is based on facts that can be verified and that a HOT thought is based on judgments, opinions or prejudices.
- Realizing that how I think influences how I feel, and that how I feel influences my decisions and my behavior.

1b. USEFULNESS OF THE SKILL

If I am aware that there are two ways of thinking, HOT and COOL, I know that my state of mind and my feelings depend mainly on me (on my thoughts) and not on events that happen in my life.

This means that my happiness does not depend on factors I cannot control. I can't always change a situation, but I can always choose to think COOL and feel better, whatever the circumstances.

Viktor Frankl wrote the following about the years he spent in a Nazi concentration camp facing the threat of death every day:

> "Everything can be taken from a man
> but one thing: the last of the human freedoms –
> to choose one's attitude in any given
> set of circumstances."
>
> **Viktor Frankl**
> *Man's Search for Meaning*

1c. MATERIALS

- Chalk for drawing a line
- Cards (see end of chapter):
  HOT, COOL
  SITUATION-THOUGHT-EMOTION
  IS WHAT I AM THINKING ABSOLUTELY TRUE?
  DOES IT HELP ME IF I THINK LIKE THIS?
- Two small cards (red and blue), one of each for each person
- A small ball
- List of HOT and COOL thoughts

2. INTRODUCTION/REVIEW OF PREVIOUS SKILLS

Later, in the following workshops, the skills learned in previous sessions are reviewed here in order to see if the previous skills have been well understood and are being put into practice. As this is the first workshop, there is no review of previous skills at this point.

So, instead of a review, the parent could start by saying something like, "Let's do some fun activities and learn about our emotions and how to be in control of them." Later on, we can learn how to identify them, how to calm down when we want to be calmer, how to feel good about ourselves, improve our relationships with other people, resolve problems and conflicts, and overcome our various challenges more easily.

Let's try an activity!

3. ACTIVITY: HOT AND COOL THOUGHTS

A - Write "SITUATION (what happens)" on the top left side of a board or large sheet of paper:

SITUATION (what happens)

We now ask if anyone would like to comment on a situation that was difficult for them, and a child might say, "I got a bad mark," and we write it down on the board under the heading "SITUATION."

So, now we have:

SITUATION
I got a bad mark

B - Now we add the word "EMOTION" at the top of the board on the far right:

SITUATION	EMOTION
I got a bad mark	

And we ask, "How did that make you feel?"

The answer might be "angry," and we write the answer under the new heading "EMOTION."

So, now we have:

SITUATION	EMOTION
I got a bad mark	*Anger*

C - Now we write "THOUGHT" on the board at the top, in the middle.

We ask, "What did you think about what happened?"

And we write the main thought in the middle column. For example, "It makes me look like an idiot."

So, now we have:

SITUATION	THOUGHT	EMOTION
I got a bad mark	*It makes me look like like an idiot*	*Anger*

And then we say: You got a bad mark on the exam, you thought it made you look like an idiot, and you felt angry! Would you like to feel better about it?

Let's see what happens if you change the way you think. For example, if you think: "I don't like it, but I'm not an idiot," how would you feel?

And the answer is "Not so bad."

Now we can say: So, the way we think affects the way we feel. Right?

And: Did you know that there are two very different ways we can think? One way we think makes us feel bad or worse, and it's called HOT thinking. The other way we think is called COOL thinking and it makes us feel good, or better. Now we place a card that says HOT and a card that says COOL side by side on the board under the heading "THOUGHT" or we write HOT and COOL on the board.

SITUATION	THOUGHT		EMOTION
	HOT	COOL	

And we move on to some more examples:
Supposing we think, "I'm never going to get a good grade."
If I think like that, how do I feel?
The answer might be "Worried."
And we write the answer on the board under the heading "EMOTION."
Then we can ask: What happens if we change this thought and if we think, for example, "It's not true that I will never get a good grade. I can always ask for help, I can make more effort, and I can have a better chance of getting a good grade."
So, now we ask: Thinking like that, would we feel worried?
And the answer is maybe concerned, or even optimistic, rather than worried.
And we continue discussing a variety of situations and thoughts, and we write down the emotions that arise on

the board under the heading "EMOTIONS."
We give different situations to parents as well and ask how they feel. Parents are learning along with the children, and their active participation helps the children to learn.

Examples of some children's situations:

- The teacher has left you without a break.
- Someone has taken the ball from you.
- You are enjoying yourself.
- Someone bumps into you, and you fall and hurt yourself.
- Your friends are playing without you.
- It's raining and you don't have an umbrella.
- You played with your friends.
- You are not first in line.
- You have homework to do.

Once everyone has understood the difference between HOT and COOL thoughts, we play the HOT and COOL game.

THE HOT AND COOL GAME

You draw a line on the floor and create a side for thoughts that are HOT and a side for thoughts that are COOL.

The Game:
You show a card with a thought written on it (see the Materials section, at the end of the chapter), or you say the thought out loud, and the children run to one side of the line or the other according to whether they think that the thought is HOT or COOL. It is a good idea to move from one

thought to the next fairly quickly in order to create a sense of expectation and excitement.

Sometimes there is disagreement on whether the thought is HOT or COOL and some children go to one side while others go to the other. If that happens, you can ask them to explain why they have gone to the side they have chosen and encourage an exchange of opinions about why they think that the thought is HOT or why it is COOL. Sometimes a thought can have different interpretations. Sometimes, based on reflection, children will change their opinion and switch sides.

Now you can reverse roles and the children choose the cards and hold them up, and the parents go to one side or the other!

An alternative game with red and blue cards for older children

You distribute two colored cards (red and blue) to each person and, when you show a card with a thought on it, or when you say the thought out loud, the children hold up one of their cards — red for a HOT thought and blue for a COOL thought.

Again, sometimes it is not obvious if a thought is HOT or COOL, and some children will raise their red card and others their blue card. If this happens, it is an ideal time to encourage a discussion in order to better identify the differences between HOT and COOL thoughts.

4. REFLECTIONS

Some notes on this topic:

1. When we change our thoughts from HOT to COOL, it is important to understand that we are not suppressing our emotions but rather being in control of them by choosing how we think.
2. Choosing to think HOT or COOL is a decision for each person, whether child or adult. It is not for others to say that someone has to think in a particular way.
3. As thinking COOL is based on facts rather than opinions, it is important that the difference between facts and opinions is understood. A fact is something that can be proven to be true with evidence (for example there are seven days in a week); an opinion is a belief and cannot be proved in the same way (for example, "This is the best chocolate in the world").
4. One of the great benefits of COOL thinking is that, although we can't always change a situation, we can always change our thoughts!

5. WHAT HAVE WE LEARNED TODAY? USEFULNESS OF THE SKILL

Here everyone can reflect on:

- The two ways of thinking are: HOT and COOL.
- If we think HOT, we feel worse. Thinking COOL helps us feel better.
- This means that we have the power to change how we feel.

And regarding the usefulness of the skill:

- Does it help us to know that we can decide whether

to think COOL instead of HOT and be in charge of how we feel?
- Does it also help us make better decisions, act in a more appropriate way and achieve our goals more easily?

6. CONSCIOUS BREATHING

If you have not done conscious breathing before, don't worry! In our daily lives many, or most, of us do not make time for ourselves. By dedicating a few moments to breathing consciously, for one minute at first, and then gradually building up to five or ten minutes or more, we create a space for ourselves to turn inwards and away from the outside world.

When doing this as a family, choose a moment when you can all take a short break. Sit somewhere you feel comfortable. Make sure that the phone will not disturb you. Make sure the light is not too bright.

If you have downloaded the Cool is Best app, you will find an audio recording for Skill 1 that you can listen to if you wish.

Before beginning, explain:

We are going to breathe normally, without making any effort. The only different thing we are going to do is to pay attention to our breathing, nothing more. This is called conscious breathing or mindful breathing, that is, being aware of our breathing as we breathe.

We are going to close our eyes to focus our attention on our breathing.

So now you say:

Let's sit in a comfortable position with our eyes closed,

our backs straight, our shoulders back in an open position and our feet in contact with the ground, without crossing our legs.

We put one hand on our stomach and the other on our chest and we notice that our body is moving, and that it is moving because of our breathing.

We have nothing else to do right now, we just focus our attention on our breathing. We focus our attention on the here and now, in the present moment.

We continue to breathe, each of us at our own pace. We focus our attention on our breathing. If any thought or concern arises, it doesn't matter. When we become aware of it, we will simply turn our attention back to our breathing. If we like, we can imagine transforming the thought into a bird and letting it fly away.

Now, while we continue to breathe, we also put our attention on our feet, and on their contact with the ground. We are going to feel very relaxed and heavy. This sensation goes up our legs, our knees. Our legs feel very relaxed and heavy. This sensation rises up our body, the lower part of the back and the stomach. We feel all these areas very relaxed, and we feel the pleasant sensation that relaxation gives us.

This relaxed, heavy sensation goes up the chest, the back, the shoulders. It goes down the arms and reaches the hands, which become very relaxed and heavy. The relaxation goes up the neck, the head, and reaches the eyes, the eyelids and the lips. We feel our whole body very relaxed and heavy. We continue to breathe, and we feel like our whole body is breathing.

Now, let's turn our attention to the thoughts that may come to our minds. We are not our thoughts. If our thoughts help us, we take note of them. But if they don't help us, we observe them and let them disappear. We have control over what we think, so we have control over how we feel. We think about that a moment: We are in control of our emotions, the most important part of our life!

A brief pause.

We take a deep breath, calmly and without exaggeration. A second. And a third. And little by little we will move our toes, our bodies, our fingers, and we open our eyes.

After pausing a moment, we can talk about how the conscious breathing went. How did we feel? What did we notice?

If some of us have difficulties, we can talk about them and remind ourselves that conscious breathing, like any skill, gets easier with practice.

We can recommend finding a regular time of day to practice breathing during the week because it will be easier if we always practice at the same time.

7. WHAT TO DO BETWEEN SESSIONS

You can suggest that between workshops we all:

- be more aware of how we feel and what we think during the week.
- practice thinking COOL.
- practice changing our thoughts from HOT to COOL.
- practice conscious breathing.

You can also suggest keeping a diary to keep track of HOT and COOL thoughts. Children especially, but also adults, will find it easier to remember their thoughts if they make a record of them.

8. MATERIALS FOR USE DURING THE ACTIVITIES

Situation / Event
What happens

Thought
What I think

Emotion
How I feel

COOL

HOT

Does it help me to think like this?

Is what I am thinking absolutely true?

SOME THOUGHTS FOR THE HOT AND COOL GAME

HOT THOUGHTS	COOL THOUGHTS
Bad things always happen to me.	It's not true that bad things always happen to me.
Today is the worst day of my life.	Today didn't go well, but it's not that bad.
I have to be perfect.	I can make mistakes.
I have to be the best.	I will do my best.
If I don't do everything right, I'm no good.	Everybody makes mistakes.
I can't make mistakes.	If I make mistakes, I can learn from them.
If I ask for help, everyone will think I'm stupid.	It's a good thing to ask for help if I need it.
If I make a mistake, they will laugh at me.	If I make mistakes, I can learn from them.
If it doesn't work out, it's the end of the world.	Some things will work out better than others.
Everything I do ends badly.	Sometimes things turn out badly but not always.
My bike doesn't work and it's raining, what a disaster.	I don't like this but it's not that bad.
If you don't listen to me, you're not my friend.	Sometimes my friends won't have time to talk with me.
My friends always have to play with me.	My friends can play with anyone they want.
If we don't play the game I want, I'm not going to play.	I'll try anything.
If I don't get what I want, life is a pain.	It's OK if I don't always get what I want.

HOW DID THE ACTIVITIES GO?

Maybe they went really well. Or maybe you didn't find it so easy. If that was the case, don't be discouraged! These things can take time. And, of course, a lot depends on the ages of your children and your own emotional state. Try to focus on the fact that practicing this skill will be of enormous benefit to you and your children now and in the future. You will all have better control of your thoughts and feelings if you can make this a regular practice.

But remember: Avoid being demanding towards yourself or others!

QUESTIONNAIRE SKILL 1

KEY:
4-Totally Agree
3-Agree
2-Disagree
1-Totally Disagree

NOTE: Put a circle around the number of your reply.

a. Now I am aware of how I can handle my emotions better by thinking COOL.
1— 2 — 3 — 4

b. It is useful to know that thinking COOL helps me manage my emotions and that thinking HOT makes it more difficult.
1— 2 — 3 — 4

c. I see that thinking COOL helps me make better decisions. **1— 2 — 3 — 4**

d. I would recommend this skill to my friends. **1— 2 — 3 — 4**

SKILL 2

RECOGNIZING OUR EMOTIONS
Being Comfortable Expressing How We Feel

When we learn to identify and talk about our emotions, we are able to let other people know how we feel and they are consequently able to take our feelings into account in the process of finding satisfactory outcomes to problems that may arise. Furthermore, when others listen to us with empathy (see Skill 4), our feelings are likely to become less intense and consequently less likely to turn into grudges or grievances that may become a reason for estranging at some point.

The universality of emotions

According to the research of the psychologist Paul Ekman, six emotions are expressed worldwide almost regardless of culture: joy, sadness, fear, anger, disgust and surprise.

We all have the same emotions

It is common for us to think that we are the only ones to feel the way we do, but in fact we all experience the same emotions and we all express them at different times with differing levels of intensity (see Skill 1). It is extremely useful to know this because knowing it helps us to be accepting of our own emotions and to express them without feeling shame, as well as to have empathy for others (see Skill 4).

Emotions are neither good nor bad and each one has a particular function

Emotions are more or less pleasant or unpleasant, rather than good or bad. They are both useful and necessary and play an essential role in our lives. It is impossible to imagine life without emotions, as they are a constant part of our daily experiences and give meaning to them. They give us the energy to act in the different situations that arise in our lives and each one has a particular function. For example:

Fear: can help save our lives
Sadness: can help us to connect with the pain caused by something that happens in our lives and process it
Anger: can help us to defend ourselves from a threat
Joy: the expression of how we feel when everything goes the way we want

Nevertheless, our emotions can harm us if their intensity is not appropriate to the circumstances, as, for example, in excessive anger that turns people away or develops into bitterness, or excessive sadness that turns into depression.

> "I didn't want to talk, yet I did, and I liked expressing myself."
>
> **Girl, 13 years old**
> *From video at the end of Cool is Best workshop*

We do not express all of our emotions

Expressing emotions such as sadness or fear is often seen as an indication of weakness. These emotions are often regarded as either positive and acceptable (joy, surprise, love, curiosity) or negative and taboo (anger, fear, sadness, disgust), and as a result we learn to repress or deny them. It is common to be told, "Don't cry, be strong," "Don't be afraid" or "Don't be a baby." As a result, we often create a "strong," but false, image of ourselves that we have to expend energy trying to maintain.

Talking about our emotions, naming them, and feeling relief

When we talk about how we feel and can put a name to our emotions, they often become less intense. Figures in the public eye sometimes talk to the media about their struggles and about how they feel, and many of them comment that expressing their emotions gives them a sense of relief. It is common in Cool is Best workshops to see children and adults alike taking the opportunity to talk freely about their emotions (see Activities section at end of chapter).

> "I have learned that I can express how I feel and nothing bad will happen."
>
> **Girl, 9 years old**
>
> *From video at the end of Cool is Best workshop*

Learning to identify a wider range of emotions

The activity at the end of the chapter can be adapted to incorporate a wider vocabulary of emotions in order to enable children and parents to acquire and use a richer emotional vocabulary. For example:

Joy: happiness, contentment, well-being, peace of mind, enjoyment, delight
Sadness: sorrow, heartbreak, melancholy, grief, misery
Anger: annoyance, irritation, frustration, fury, rage
Fear: worry, anxiety, concern, dread, terror
Disgust: dislike, aversion, revulsion, repugnance
Surprise: amazement, wonder, marvel, astonishment
Love: affection, fondness, passion, infatuation

Emotions that can be triggered as a result of parents' own childhood experiences

Many parents have issues from their own experiences in childhood caused by a whole plethora of problems such as having had an insecure attachment to their parents, or having been badly treated, abused or bullied. These issues can cause parents to have disturbed feelings and behave in self-defeating ways when situations with their children remind them deep down of their own experiences. It is therefore important that parents are aware of where these strong feelings and reactions come from in order to be able to address and resolve them and prevent them from affecting their children. An effective way to prevent these feelings from being overwhelming is to practice conscious breathing regularly (see Skill 6). Practicing this skill enables us to take a deep, slow breath if necessary and feel calmer, just as we feel when we are in the midst of a regular practice of conscious breathing.

ACTIVITIES TO DO TOGETHER WITH YOUR CHILDREN

PARENT GUIDE: SKILL 2

RECOGNIZING MY EMOTIONS

INTRODUCTION

These activities should be adapted to the ages of the children participating and to your own parental circumstances.

If you find the Six Skills of value, you can download the Cool is Best app, where you will find additional resources including videos, audios, and interactive e-books for children from 8 to 14 years old.

Note for teachers: these activities are used successfully in Cool is Best workshops with students in school.

INDEX TO ACTIVITIES (40 MINS)

1. Objectives, usefulness, materials
2. Brief review of previous skill (5 mins)
3. Activity (20 mins)
4. Reflections (5 mins)
5. What have we learned today? The usefulness of the skill (5 mins)
6. Conscious breathing (5 mins)
7. What to do between sessions

1a. OBJECTIVES

- Recognize how I feel and name my emotions.
- Know that I'll feel better if I talk about how I feel.
- Recognize that all people have the same emotions.
- Understand that different people can experience different intensities of emotion in the face of the same event.
- See emotions as pleasant or unpleasant rather than good or bad.
- Know that even unpleasant emotions have a purpose (e.g., fear helps us avoid danger).
- Understand that my emotions affect how I behave.
- See that my behavior has consequences and therefore my emotions do too.

I practice the first steps of mindful breathing.

1b. USEFULNESS OF THE SKILL

- It is very helpful to understand that my emotions affect my behavior.
- If I have a problem, I can see that it can help me feel better if I talk about how I feel with someone else who listens well and does not judge me (see Skill 4).
- Understanding that we all have the same emotions makes it easier to understand, value, and accept the emotions of others.

1c. MATERIALS

- Die or small box with emojis of six emotions (joy, sadness, disgust, fear, anger, love) drawn on the sides
- Alternative: cards with emojis of the same six emotions (you will also need something like a bowl from which the cards will be taken)
- Markers
- Small ball

2. BRIEF REVIEW OF PREVIOUS SKILLS

Skill 1 – Managing my emotions by thinking COOL

The ball is passed to someone who is asked: what did we do last time?

You ask: Have we been more in control of our emotions by thinking COOL (Skill 1) during the week? Would anyone like to give an example?

You also ask: Have we all practiced conscious breathing during the past week, and has it helped us in some way?

3. ACTIVITY

Rolling the die (or taking a card)

We sit in a circle on chairs or on the floor.

We explain briefly that the activity is about talking about the emotions that arise in day-to-day situations. The role of those who are listening is to listen with attention and interest and to let each person talk without being interrupted.

Everyone takes a turn rolling the die (or taking a card), and when it comes to rest on an emotion, you ask the person who rolled the die if they would like to talk about a situation in which they felt the emotion, how intense it was and how the emotion affected their behavior.

If some prefer not to talk, that's fine, there is no obligation; they will learn by watching the others and may ask to have their turn later.

A sense of anticipation often arises as each person rolls the die: what is going to be the emotion this time? And when the die settles, people are often keen to recount an experience in which they felt the emotion. The number of times each person rolls the die is something that can be decided by you and the other participants, and you can do the activity as many times as you all like both during the workshop and at other times.

At the end of the activity, it is always a great idea to thank everyone for their participation and contributions.

Talking about a difficult experience

Although the idea of the activity is to talk about day-to-day situations that don't have a great emotional impact, sometimes people talk about experiences that have greatly affected them (for example, the death of a pet). If this happens, it is important to listen and give full attention to the speaker, and then say something like, "Oh, that is so sad (or painful, or frightening)" so that the speaker feels listened to and validated (see Skill 4 for more on empathic listening). Also ask the listeners if they have experienced similar situations or emotions so that the speaker sees that they are not alone in having those feelings.

4. REFLECTIONS

At the end of the activity, you can ask if there are any comments and you can also ask questions to encourage reflection, such as:

- Can we imagine a day without emotions, given that emotions are such an important part of our lives?
- What is an emotion?
- Can we put a name to our emotions?
- Have we noticed how our emotions affect our behavior?
- Do our behaviors have consequences? Can we give examples?
- Do we all have the same emotions?
- Do emotions have different intensities?
- What was it like to talk about how we feel?
- Does it help us if we talk about how we feel? Why?
- Is it important that we talk about how we feel with a trusted person who will listen to us?
- Do we agree that unpleasant emotions are neither good nor bad? For example, fear can help save my life and sadness helps us overcome loss.

5. WHAT HAVE WE LEARNED TODAY? USEFULNESS OF THE SKILL

Some examples of things that you and your children might talk about:

- Being more aware of our emotions.
- Being aware that we all have the same emotions

and that we are not alone in feeling uncomfortable emotions.
- Realizing that it is useful to talk about how we feel because expressing our emotions can help us to feel better, or less bad.

6. CONSCIOUS BREATHING

If you have downloaded the Cool is Best app, you will find an audio recording for Skill 2 that you can listen to if you wish.

Before beginning, explain:

We are going to breathe normally, without making any effort. The only different thing we are going to do is pay attention to our breathing, nothing more. This is called conscious breathing or mindful breathing, that is, being aware of our breathing as we breathe. We are going to close our eyes and focus our attention on our breathing.

Now you say:

Let's sit in a comfortable position with our eyes closed, our backs straight, our shoulders back in an open position and our feet in contact with the ground, without crossing our legs.

We put one hand on our stomach and the other on our chest, and we notice that our body is moving, and that it is moving because of our breathing.

We have nothing else to do right now, we just focus our attention on our breathing. We focus our attention on the here and now, in the present moment.

We continue to breathe, each of us at our own pace. We focus our attention on our breathing. If any thought or concern arises, it doesn't matter. When we become aware of it, we will simply turn our attention back to our breathing. If we like, we can imagine transforming the thought into a bird and letting it fly away.

Now, while we continue to breathe, we also put our attention on our feet, and on their contact with the ground. We are going to feel very relaxed and heavy. This sensation goes up our legs, our knees. Our legs feel very relaxed and heavy. This sensation rises up our body, the lower part of the back, and the stomach. We feel all these areas become very relaxed, and we feel the pleasant sensation that relaxation gives us.

This relaxed, heavy sensation goes up the chest, the back, the shoulders. It goes down the arms and reaches the hands, which become very relaxed and heavy. The relaxation goes up the neck, the head, and reaches the eyes, the eyelids and the lips. We feel our whole body very relaxed and heavy. We continue to breathe, and we feel like our whole body is breathing.

From this state of relaxation, we give our attention to **how we feel, to our emotions**. Do we feel happy? Regretful? Fearful? Anxious? Grateful? Nervous? How strong is the intensity? Is it low or high? Or in the middle? Whatever we feel, we accept it. We say to ourselves: This is how I feel right now, and I accept it. I recognize that everyone has the same feelings at different times, so I am not alone in having these feelings. If I want to, I can find someone I trust and tell them how I feel, and that will help me.

We continue to breathe, paying attention to our

breathing. We take a deep breath, calmly and without exaggeration. A second breath. A third. And little by little we move our toes, our fingers, our bodies, and we open our eyes.

After pausing a moment, we can talk about how the conscious breathing went. How did we feel? What did we notice? Have we practiced during the week?

If some of us have difficulties, we can talk about them and remind ourselves that conscious breathing, like any skill, gets easier with practice.

We can recommend finding a time of day during the week to practice (it is best if it is always at the same time).

7. WHAT TO DO BETWEEN SESSIONS

Suggest that between workshops:

- We try to be aware of how we feel and how intense our emotions are, whether they are mild, medium or strong.
- We practice conscious breathing regularly.

HOW DID THE ACTIVITIES GO?

Maybe they went really well, and you are happy with how they went.

Or maybe you didn't find it so easy. If that was the case, don't be discouraged! These things can take time. And of course, a lot depends on the ages of your children. And your own emotional situation. So just focus on the fact that practicing Skills 1 and 2 will be of enormous benefit for you and your children, now and in the future, and find a way that works for you to put them into practice.

QUESTIONNAIRE SKILL 2

KEY:
4-Totally Agree
3-Agree
2-Disagree
1-Totally Disagree

NOTE: Put a circle around the number of your reply.

a. Now I am more aware of my emotions.
1— 2 — 3 — 4
b. Now I am more aware of the emotions of others.
1— 2 — 3 — 4
c. Being aware of my emotions helps me. For example, if I'm aware that I'm feeling angry, I can put off making decisions until I feel calmer.
1— 2 — 3 — 4
d. It helps me to know that I am not the only one who has strong feelings.
1— 2 — 3 — 4
e. I would recommend this skill to my friends.
1— 2 — 3 — 4

SKILL 3

HAVING HEALTHY SELF-ESTEEM
Feeling Good About
Ourselves and Others

We have healthy self-esteem when we accept and value ourselves just as we are, and we do this by thinking COOL thoughts (Skill 1) about ourselves. When we fully accept ourselves, with all those aspects that we like and all those that we don't like so much, we feel good about ourselves and are able to more easily accept others as they are. As a result, we will be more tolerant and less likely to want to hurt others or estrange from them. Having healthy self-esteem also means that if others treat us badly, their behavior will not affect us, or will not affect us as much.

Self-esteem: Internal and external factors

There is a common misconception that self-esteem depends on having possessions, friends and successes. But if we base our self-esteem on these things, our feelings about ourselves will fluctuate according to what happens in our lives. If, on the other hand, our self-esteem depends on how we think about ourselves, we can think COOL thoughts, accept ourselves and feel good about ourselves, whatever our circumstances. And if we feel good about ourselves, we are more likely to make the effort required to achieve our goals in life and to flourish.

When we are children, our sense of self-worth largely comes from how we are treated by others, especially our parents. If our parents or those caring for us treat us with love, listen to us, appreciate how things are from our point of view, understand us and are accepting towards us, we learn to value and accept ourselves. Part of this approach involves discussing with children any rules that parents may think necessary. When children are involved in making the rules, they will be far less likely to break them. Nobody likes having rules imposed on them. To take into account the possibility that rules that have been agreed upon are not adhered to, it is important to have a procedure for resolving this type of problem. It is vital that parents do not punish, blame, or put down their children, or treat one child more favorably than another. These experiences hurt children's self-esteem, have long-lasting adverse effects and may well cause resentment in the future.

As children grow older it is important that their self-esteem comes more and more from the way they think about themselves and that they no longer depend on outside factors; in adults, healthy self-esteem comes from within. Self-esteem, like any skill, is something that can be worked on and improved.

Some COOL thoughts that help me believe in myself, feel good, and have healthy self-esteem:

- "I accept myself just as I am, with all the things that I like about myself and all the things that I do not like so much."
- "If people treat me disrespectfully, I see that as a reflection on them, not on me."
- "I am not here to fulfill the expectations of other people, although I am happy to do my best to find satisfactory outcomes for everyone concerned."
- "I will try hard, but if I do not succeed, I will value myself just as much."
- "I will do my best — rather than demand that I do things perfectly."

Self-acceptance

Albert Ellis (see Skill 1) advocated that we give ourselves "USA" (unconditional self-acceptance) and accept ourselves simply because we exist, regardless of what we do or what we have or whom we know. However, we should nevertheless behave in a moral way.

> "I feel better."
>
> **Girl, 9 years old**
>
> *From video at the end of Cool is Best workshop*

Unconditional personal regard (UPR)

Unconditional personal regard means being accepting of others regardless of what they say or do. Carl Rogers, who was voted the most influential psychologist in the U.S. by The American Psychological Association for his work on active and empathic listening, maintained that treating children with UPR is the factor that most predicts their future psychological wellbeing. A 2015 study confirmed this to be the case and called the effects of treating children with "conditional regard" as "devastating." Relating to children with UPR does not mean that there are no limits. If a child behaves in unacceptable ways, parents can address the behavior but not criticise the child as a person. For example, "I don't like the way you behaved" rather than "You are a naughty boy."

What we think of ourselves is much more important than what other people think of us, contrary to what many people think

Many people think that what others think of them is paramount, but what we think of ourselves is much more important than what others think of us. If we accept and value ourselves as we are, we will not be affected by what others think or say about us, or we will not be affected as much, because we no longer depend on others for validation or approval. At the same time, we can stop comparing ourselves with others.

If I accept myself just as I am, I feel good about myself, and nothing anybody says will make me feel bad, worthless or guilty

Accepting ourselves is at the heart of our happiness and success. When we accept ourselves, we can be confident and assertive (see chapter 5), stand up for our rights, take risks, give ourselves permission to try out new things, and live life to the fullest.

Praise

Our goal is to have strong self-esteem that is also realistic. When kids do something well, rather than praise them, we can encourage and motivate them by saying something like: "Wow, I bet you were pleased with that," a response that shows that we have noticed and are interested but that does not create a dependency on outside validation.

Tolerance

If we are able to accept what we don't like about ourselves, we will be better able to accept what we don't like about others. We will have more tolerance towards them and will be better able to celebrate difference and diversity.

When we recognize and value our own capabilities, we are better able to recognize and value the capabilities of others, and we will have no need to devalue or belittle them. When we feel good about ourselves, we are able to treat others well and with kindness.

Put-down thinking — thinking I'm a failure, or that someone else is no good, or that life itself is rotten

Putting down or discounting happens when we think that we are no good and that we are a failure, or that another person is no good or that life itself is rotten or hopeless. As a result, we may think, "I did badly and therefore I am a failure" and then feel low, dispirited or depressed. Put-down thinking often follows thinking in a *demanding* way. In *How to Raise an Emotionally Healthy Happy Child*, Albert Ellis explains that if children demand of themselves that they do everything well or demand that they do better than others in order to feel good about themselves, they are likely to put themselves down and feel as if they are worth little if they do not live up to their own expectations. As a result, they may lose confidence, feel anxious, perform less well and discount themselves even more, and they may also treat others badly in order to feel better themselves.

A person may seem to have everything but nevertheless feel worthless and, to alleviate their distress, criticize a family member for things that happened many years ago and then estrange from them.

Labeling

If you call yourself a failure, challenge your thinking. You are not a failure just because something didn't go as well as you had hoped. Try out new thoughts that are both true and helpful.

If you have said to yourself that you are a failure because you didn't do something well, an alternative helpful thought could be, "It doesn't make sense for me to *demand* that I do it well and to call myself a failure if I don't do it well. I am more than that."

Try finishing these sentences:

If I tell myself I am a failure, then

____

If I tell myself I did my best, then

____

Projecting

If I do not accept myself, I may project, that is, criticize others for the very things that I am, or have done, or have caused myself.

Joanna accused her brother of not caring about her family, yet, according to her brother, he did care and had always been happy to meet up with them. Moreover, he had never made critical comments about them, whereas his sister had been contemptuous of his own spouse and had even questioned her veracity on several occasions. The sister's accusation was simply a projection: she accused her brother of the very thing that she herself had done.

I do not need the approval of others — though I do my best to have good relationships with them

I like it when other people appreciate me and accept me and love me, but I do not *need* others to approve of me in order to feel good about myself. This means I do not need to care too much what other people think of me.

I am the one who makes me happy, and no one else has the responsibility for doing that. This is my life! That means that I don't make excuses, and I don't blame events or other people for things that happen to me, nor do I let others make me feel inadequate, guilty or ashamed. Nonetheless, I am happy to accept appreciation from others, in the same way that I enjoy giving appreciation to them myself.

Just as I am responsible for my own life, others are responsible for their lives — their thoughts, their feelings, their behaviors and their happiness. When they have problems, I do my best to put myself in their shoes and listen to them with empathy and compassion and to be supportive (Skill 4).

Other people have their impression of me, but it is unlikely to be fully accurate because I am changing and developing all the time and they may have misunderstood something, or they may be prejudiced and unable or unwilling to see the whole me.

If they attack me unfairly, I see that *they* are the ones that have the problem but, because I feel good about myself, I nevertheless wish them well. Here is an extreme example of this:

"I am not angry with you...I don't think you owe me an apology...I wish you well."

Dr. Adam Towler of Bristol, England

Dr. Towler was stabbed nine times by a deranged youth in a random attack and almost died.
BBC News 2022

Accepting myself as I am does not mean resigning myself

If we accept ourselves as we are, it does not mean that we cannot change if we want to. For example, if I want to have good relationships with other people, I can work to improve my listening and communication skills and be proud of myself for doing my best.

The important thing is that *we* are the ones who decide if we want to change. We are the only ones responsible for changing ourselves and for valuing ourselves. This can be challenging but we make sure that we do not submit to any pressure that society or others may exert on us.

Nowadays, because of social media, we focus more attention than ever on physical appearance which leads to our comparing ourselves to others. Reality shows make cosmetic surgery seem like an easy way to change one's appearance, but they do not show that the effectiveness of surgery has a limited life and often makes matters worse over time. Would we not do better learning to accept and love ourselves as we are?

Making mistakes is normal, and mistakes benefit me if I learn from them

When we make mistakes, we may put ourselves down and feel ashamed or guilty, or we may avoid trying new things out of fear of failure. But making mistakes helps us because we can learn important lessons from our failures. Little children make mistakes as they learn to walk and to speak, but they carry on trying until they master the skills!

It is normal to make mistakes — everybody makes mistakes! Indeed, people who are more open to learning and more willing to try new things probably make more mistakes than those who never try anything new. Therefore, I remind myself that making mistakes shows that I am growing and learning, and I do not give myself a hard time when things don't work out.

How we feel when we make mistakes largely depends on the way we think. If we think, "I always try my best and it's not a problem if I make mistakes because they will help me learn," making mistakes will not adversely affect our self-esteem. We may feel frustrated if we make repeated mistakes, as a child does when learning to ride a bike, but we can assure ourselves that, just like that child, if we stick with our new activity, we will master it. We know our mistakes do not make us failures.

To put failure in perspective, here is what Thomas Edison, one of many inventors who worked to make the light bulb economically viable during the late 19th century, said about failure:

> **"I have not failed. I have just found 1,000 ways that do not work."**
>
> **Thomas Edison**
>
> *Inventor who spent many years trying to make the light bulb commercially viable.*

Taking responsibility for myself

When I see that I have poor results or have behaved in a way I am not proud of, I take responsibility for my actions and do my best to improve and put things right. I do not search for others to blame!

Because I believe in myself, I am able to set myself realistic short- and long-term goals and be confident that I can achieve them. I am able to accurately assess my own strengths, weaknesses and limitations, and make improvements if I judge them to be necessary.

Some of the goals I set are easy and some are challenging; some are short-term, and some are long-term. However, my goals are realistic, and if circumstances change, I can adjust them. In any case, I carry them out with persistence and without giving up when I come across obstacles. Having healthy self-esteem and the ability to tolerate frustration through COOL thinking helps me to achieve this.

Being accepting of others

Being accepting of others is enormously beneficial. Acceptance prevents us from becoming upset by other people, resentful towards them, angry at them or wanting to fight or hurt them. Acceptance helps us relate to people whose actions we don't like and may even help us influence them.

A helpful thought to have here is:

> "Nobody is here to fulfill my expectations,
> and even less so my demands."

To develop acceptance of others, look at any thoughts and beliefs you have that imply that other people are not acceptable, and practice the COOL thought that "I accept other people exactly as they are, even if I do not like what they do sometimes." You may add: "If they do something I don't like, I will not put them down or insult them just because they are not perfect, and I will let them be who they are." This does not mean that we should let other people treat us badly. We can criticize and object to their actions but avoid calling them a bad person.

> "I recognize that these skills will create well-being in me and, at the same time, this will generate well-being in those around me."
>
> **A teacher**
>
> *From video at end of Cool is Best workshops*

Being accepting of life

Being accepting of life is an attitude that allows you to be relaxed about whatever happens, especially things over which you have no control. Being accepting does not mean that you can't do everything possible to make changes if you want things to be different in the future; it just means you are able to accept things as they are right now.

In order to develop an attitude of acceptance, realize that there will always be problems and that you can bear them and even overcome them with effort. When things happen that you cannot change, you can choose to be accepting and therefore feel more at ease, while at the same time planning your next steps.

Living authentically

If we accept ourselves as we are, we have no need to pretend to be different than we are. We have no need to create a mask in order to prevent others from seeing who we really are.

Being authentic means we do not fake who we are in order to be liked or accepted. When our behavior is congruent with our values, we live authentically and have integrity. We do not do things simply to please others.

> "Esse Quam Videri" ("Be What You Seem")
>
> **Motto of Berklee College of Music, Boston**

Thoughts and affirmations of people with healthy self-esteem

I believe in myself and accept myself unconditionally and I have the right to:

- be happy and enjoy life
- say and ask for what I want and negotiate for it and defend my rights

- express my feelings, opinions and desires
- make my own decisions and reject the advice of others if I so decide
- say no without having to justify myself
- make mistakes and not do everything perfectly
- be treated with respect
- not be taken advantage of
- question unfairness rather than just put up with it
- change my mind and renegotiate something that was previously agreed upon

At the same time, I have the duty to:

- be in control of myself emotionally
- think and express myself in a way that is helpful
- take responsibility for myself and my actions
- respect other people's rights, needs and desires
- be clear when expressing myself
- not judge or blame others
- try to find win-win solutions to problems and conflicts (see chapter 5)

ACTIVITIES TO DO TOGETHER WITH YOUR CHILDREN

PARENT GUIDE: SKILL 3

HAVING HEALTHY SELF-ESTEEM

INTRODUCTION

These activities should be adapted to the ages of the children participating and to your own parental circumstances.

If you find the Six Skills of value, you can download the Cool is Best app, where you will find additional resources including videos, audios, and interactive e-books for children from 8 to 14 years old.

Note for teachers: these activities are used successfully in Cool is Best workshops with students in school.

INDEX (40 MINS)

1. Objectives, usefulness, materials
2. Brief review of previous workshops (5 mins)
3. Activity (20 mins)
4. Reflections (5 mins)
5. What have we learned today? The usefulness of the skill (5 mins)
6. Conscious breathing (5 mins)
7. What to do between sessions

1a. OBJECTIVES

- Understand that having self-esteem depends on the way I think about myself. I have healthy self-esteem if I value and accept myself as I am (i.e., I think COOL about myself), and I don't have strong self-esteem if I belittle myself by thinking HOT thoughts about myself.
- Understand that my self-esteem is the evaluation I make of myself and that I have healthy self-esteem if I feel good about myself.
- Understand the benefits of accepting myself just as I am and know that accepting myself helps me be more accepting of others.

1b. USEFULNESS OF THE SKILL

- If I feel good about myself, I can establish good relationships with others, will have no need to be unkind and can achieve my personal goals more easily.
- If I feel good about myself and accept myself as I am, it doesn't affect me if other people say negative things about me, or it doesn't affect me as much.

1c. MATERIALS

- A4 paper
- Post-it Notes or small sheets of paper (10x10 cm.)
- Adhesive or Blu-Tack
- Markers
- Small ball

2. BRIEF REVIEW OF PREVIOUS SKILLS

We pass the ball (optional) and the person with the ball speaks if they wish.

Skill 1 – Managing my emotions by thinking COOL
Have we been aware of our HOT thoughts and COOL thoughts? Have we put into practice changing our HOT thoughts to COOL? And seen how our feelings change?

Skill 2 – Recognizing my emotions
Have we been more aware of our emotions, and can we name them and give examples?

Conscious breathing
Have we practiced? How did it go?

3. ACTIVITY: WHAT WE LIKE AND LIKE LESS ABOUT OURSELVES

We distribute four Post-it Notes or four small pieces of paper, which can be colored during the activity and each of us writes down two things that we like about ourselves and two things that we don't like as much or might like to improve.

We can give examples such as I am a good friend, I am shy, impatient, jealous, and so on.

It is important to note that this activity it is not about saying "I like playing football," or "I don't like salad," but rather writing something about our characteristics or personality. When we are finished writing, we glue the Post-it Notes onto larger individual white sheets of paper and talk about what we have written. This is, of course, voluntary for everyone. At the end of the activity, we put the Post-it Notes up on the wall.

4. REFLECTIONS

We talk about what we wrote and see that healthy self-esteem means accepting and valuing both the things we like about ourselves and the things we don't like as much, and as a result, feeling good about ourselves.

Putting ourselves down

- Are we aware of it when we have automatic HOT thoughts about ourselves and judge ourselves and make unreasonable demands on ourselves?
- Say out loud in a strong voice: "I have the right to be who I am." Can we do that?

Accepting myself as I am, including what I don't like as much about myself

- Let's imagine that I don't accept that I have a certain characteristic I don't like and that someone refers to this characteristic in an unpleasant way; how am I going to feel?
- Now let's imagine that I have accepted this characteristic unconditionally and this person makes their comment; how am I going to feel now? Better in the second case?
- We often attach great importance to what others say and think of us, but isn't what we think about ourselves much more important than what others think about us?

- Does accepting myself as I am give me peace?

Does accepting myself mean resigning myself?

We can accept ourselves, but we don't have to resign ourselves. There are many things that we can improve, but *we* are the ones who decide. For example, *I* am the one who decides if I am going to make an effort to achieve the things I want in my life. I am the only one responsible for myself. Of course, parents have an important role during the early years, but it gradually reduces as the years pass. This is a difficult role requiring parents to guide their children with care and at the same time avoid the creation of bad feelings. Rather than demanding that we be perfect, we can be happy doing the best we can (see Skill 1)!

Things that are not in our hands to improve or change

If I don't like the color of my eyes, that is something I can't change, but what I can do is accept that the color of my eyes is the way it is, even if I don't like it. Accepting myself as I am will give me peace of mind. Is that true?

What makes me feel good about myself?

- My achievements?
- My possessions?
- Money?
- My friends?

But will we always have achievements, possessions, money or friends? Or can all of these disappear? If this happens, what happens to my self-esteem?

The answer is that my self-esteem depends on the way I

think about myself. It depends on me and not on external things.

I can lose everything and still feel good about myself, and still therefore be able to make the effort I need to get back what I lost, if that is what I want to do.

5. WHAT HAVE WE LEARNED TODAY? USEFULNESS OF THE SKILL

We can emphasize the two or three most important points:

- Thinking COOL about ourselves helps us to feel good about ourselves.
- We are all a mixture of things we like and things we like less.
- If we think COOL about ourselves, accept and value ourselves and don't put ourselves down, we are more likely to have better relationships with other people.
- If I feel good about myself, I will have no need to put others down.
- If I feel good about myself, I am happy, I can make better decisions, and I can dedicate myself to my goals in life.

Above all, who is responsible for making me happy? Me!

6. CONSCIOUS BREATHING

If you have downloaded the Cool is Best app, you will find an audio recording for Skill 3 that you can listen to if you wish.

Let's sit in a comfortable position with our eyes closed, our backs straight, our shoulders back in an open position and our feet in contact with the ground, without crossing our legs.

We put one hand on our stomach and the other on our chest, and we notice that our body is moving, and that it is moving because of our breathing.

We have nothing else to do right now, we just focus our attention on our breathing. We focus our attention on the here and now, in the present moment.

We continue to breathe, each of us at our own pace. We focus our attention on our breathing. If any thought or concern arises, it doesn't matter. When we become aware of it, we will simply turn our attention back to our breathing. If we like, we can transform the thought into a bird and let it fly away.

Now, while we continue to breathe, we also put our attention on our feet and on their contact with the ground. We are going to feel very relaxed and heavy. This sensation goes up our legs. Our legs feel very relaxed and heavy. This sensation rises up our body, the lower part of the back and the stomach. We feel all these areas very relaxed, and we feel the pleasant sensation that relaxation gives us.

This relaxed, heavy sensation goes up the chest, the back, the shoulders. It goes down the arms and reaches the hands, which become very relaxed and heavy. The relaxation goes up the neck, the head, and reaches the eyes, the eyelids and the lips. We feel our whole body very relaxed and heavy. We continue to breathe, and we feel like our whole body is breathing.

Now, let's turn our attention to **how we think about**

ourselves. I accept myself and value myself. Just as I am. This way of thinking makes me feel good about myself. If I want to change something I can do it, but that is up to me and only me. I see that what I think about myself matters far more than what others think of me. As a result, if others say something unkind to me it doesn't hurt me, or it hurts me much less. If someone says something unkind, I see that it is their problem, not mine. On the other hand, if others make some constructive criticism, I will think about it and maybe make changes that will help me.

Brief pause.

We continue to breathe, paying attention to our breathing. We take a deep breath, calmly and without exaggeration. A second breath. And a third. And little by little we move our toes, our bodies, our fingers, and we open our eyes.

After pausing a moment, we can talk about how the conscious breathing went. How did we feel? What did we notice?

Have we practiced during the week?

If some of us have difficulties, we can talk about them and remind ourselves that conscious breathing, like any skill, gets easier with practice.

We can recommend finding a time of day during the week (it is better if it is always the same time) to practice.

7. WHAT TO DO BETWEEN SESSIONS

- Be aware of how we feel when we consciously accept ourselves just as we are.
- Write down something that we like about ourselves during the week.
- Do mindful breathing regularly.

HOW DID THE ACTIVITIES GO?

Maybe they went really well, and you are happy with how they went.

Or maybe you didn't find it so easy. If that was the case, don't be discouraged! These things can take time. And, of course, a lot depends on the ages of your children as well as your own emotional situation. So, just focus on the fact that practicing Skills 1, 2 and 3 will be of enormous benefit for you and your children, now and in the future, and find a way that works for you to put them into practice.

In order to keep Skills 1, 2 and 3 in mind and keep working on them, you can do the conscious breathing activity regularly and incorporate visualizations of the three skills into the text.

QUESTIONNAIRE SKILL 3

KEY:
4-Totally Agree
3-Agree
2-Disagree
1-Totally Disagree

NOTE: Put a circle around the number of your reply.

a. Now I am aware of how I can have better self-esteem by valuing myself with COOL thoughts instead of belittling myself with HOT thoughts (for example, thinking "I can do it if I try hard" instead of "I'll never be able to do it.")
1— 2 — 3 — 4

b. It helps to know that I can have better self-esteem if I think COOL about myself instead of HOT.
1— 2 — 3 — 4

c. I would recommend this skill to my friends.
1— 2 — 3 — 4

SKILL 4

LISTENING WITH EMPATHY
Creating Excellent Relationships

Listening with empathy helps us to have excellent relationships with others because, when people are listened to, heard, valued and understood, they will have good feelings towards us. Consequently, it is unlikely that they will want to estrange from us in the future.

The importance of listening is illustrated by the following story. This is only an anecdote, but, as Graham Brodie of Louisiana State University says, there are a multitude of academic studies that confirm the effectiveness of listening with empathy:

At age 17, Byron Pitts was a first-year college student, a midterm away from flunking out. One particularly memorable day began as his English professor handed back his most recent essay marked with a D+. Shortly after hearing "You are wasting my time and the government's money," Mr. Pitts began filling out the papers to withdraw from school. Fortunately for Mr. Pitts, a stranger took the time to listen and as he describes it, "She stopped. She helped me. She was encouraging, just like my mother and other people in my life, and she planted seeds of kindness in me and optimism."

THREE MAIN WAYS TO LISTEN

1. Listening with "roadblocks"

Thomas Gordon, a former doctoral student of Carl Rogers, identified what he called the common "roadblocks" to communication. When children are met with these kinds of responses, they learn that talking with parents is not helpful to them and they stop talking about their feelings. Children often complain that their parents and teachers don't understand them and that they can't get through to them. Think about how you would feel if people were to talk to you in this way:

1. "You have to do it" — ordering, directing, commanding.
2. "If you don't clean up right away..." — warning, admonishing, threatening.
3. "It would be better if..." — exhorting, moralizing, preaching.
4. "Why don't you..." — advising, giving solutions or suggestions.
5. "This makes more sense..." — lecturing, teaching, giving logical arguments.
6. "You ought to have been more careful..." — judging, criticizing, disagreeing, blaming.
7. "Well done..." — praising, so that the child comes to depend on external validation.
8. "I can think of someone else who would have done that better..." — name-calling, ridiculing, shaming, discounting.
9. "You did that because..." — interpreting, analyzing, diagnosing, jumping to conclusions.
10. "I'm sure it will turn out well in the end..." — reassuring, sympathizing, consoling.
11. "Why didn't you..." — probing, questioning, interrogating.
12. "Why don't you forget about that and go and..." — withdrawing, distracting, humoring, diverting.

These kinds of responses are likely to make both children and adults alike feel disrespected, judged, rejected or guilty and cause them to be less likely to talk about how they feel. It is true that asking questions might seem to be a response that shows interest, but questions often divert the conversation from what the other person is wanting to say.

Example

Here is an example illustrating a common way in which parents respond to children and take over a problem in order to try to help them solve it. This example shows that the child disregards his mother's advice and that his mother's approach does not help him resolve his anger.

Your son Ben comes to you and looks upset:

Ben: "Martin has taken my ball away."
Mom: "Oh, don't let that bother you (discounting/not valuing his feelings), why don't you take the other ball over there?" (offering advice and a solution).
Ben: "I don't want that other ball. I hate Martin" (strong reaction).
Mom: "Don't worry, you'll soon get over it" (trying to reassure).
Ben: "No I won't, I hate Martin and I'm never going to invite him to play again" (another strong reaction).

2. Listening with attention

This is appropriate when others do not have a problem. We listen and speak in ways that give children and others the message that we are interested in listening to what they have to say and how they feel, especially when they have something important to tell us.

You can do this by making comments such as "I see," or saying "mmm," or "aha," and by making appropriate gestures with your hands, nodding your head or making facial expressions indicating that you are listening. You can also say things such as, "Would you like to tell me anything else?" at moments that seem appropriate to you.

Everyone will have their own way of doing this, but the essential thing is to show that you are listening and do not offer your own opinions, judgments, or feelings, so that you create the conditions in which those talking are happy to keep talking.

3. Listening actively

This is appropriate when others have a problem. Active listening was first developed by the psychologist Carl Rogers and is an extraordinarily effective way of communicating when children or others have a problem. When we listen actively, we do two things: We paraphrase or summarize what others tell us about their problem and we reflect back to them how we think they feel.

> "When we listen to another person with empathy,
> that person would be able to say:
> 'He or she understands what my experience
> feels like to me.'"
>
> **Carl Rogers**
>
> *Cited in Rogers 1980:143 Barrett-Lennard 1962*

Example:

Your child is upset because some kids have made fun of him.

Mom: "The kids down the street made fun of you" (paraphrasing what was said). "That must have hurt your feelings" (reflecting how we think the child feels).

When we listen in this way, we try to understand the situation of the other person as if it were our own and we show the other person that we are listening and are interested. If we can understand what it is like to be the other person and to be in their shoes, in their actual situation, so that we understand where they have come from, we create the conditions under which we can be totally accepting towards them. As a result, they will tell us about their problem and, through talking, will often be able to find their own solution.

When you listen actively, make sure that you are in a calm emotional state. And make sure that you can handle the issue and the feelings that your children tell you about. If they tell you about something distressing, you must be able to handle it in order to be able to listen actively and keep yourself from adding anything new to what they are saying. When we listen actively, thinking in a COOL, rational and helpful way (Skill 1) is essential. If we find this difficult, we can take several breaths and focus our attention on our breathing for a moment (Skill 6).

If you do not have time to actively listen immediately, you can say when you will have time. However, if the problem is urgent and your children are very upset, it is important to make time right away if possible. A child who has had some difficult experience often feels better as if by magic as soon as their parents have truly listened to what happened!

Another example:

John says: "I have to present a report in class next week and I am going to look like an idiot."
Your possible response: "You are presenting a report next week and it sounds like you're feeling nervous about it" (paraphrasing and reflecting back the feelings).
John might then say: "Yes, I've left it too late but even if I had left myself more time, I would probably have bungled it anyway!"

Your response (think before reading the response below):

"You left it too late to prepare it well but you are not confident you would have prepared it well anyway."

___

___

___

___

John: "Yes, that's right, the fact is that it is nerve-racking to get up in front of the class, and I am not used to it."

Your response:

"I can see that you don't have practice and would feel anxious about it."

John:
"Yes, but wait a minute, how about I get myself some experience by practicing with you?" (John is beginning to find a solution).

Note that you have simply listened, paraphrased and reflected, and John has been able to talk about something that was bothering him and, although he will not always find solutions when you listen in this way, he has in this case found at least part of a solution to the problem. Bear in mind too that it is common for people to not come up with solutions immediately but to do so later after reflection, a process that will have been facilitated by your having listened actively.

THE DIFFERENCE BETWEEN LISTENING WITH ROADBLOCKS AND LISTENING ACTIVELY

Example 1

Listening with roadblocks

Ben comes to his mother looking upset:

Ben: "Martin has taken my ball away."
Mom: "Oh, don't let that bother you (minimizing feelings), why don't you take the other ball over there?" (offering advice and a solution).
Ben: "I don't want that other ball. I hate Martin" (strong reaction).
Mom: "Don't worry, you'll soon get over it" (trying to reassure).
Ben: "No, I won't, I hate Martin and I'm never going to invite him to play again" (another strong reaction).

Listening actively

Here is the same situation but with Ben's mother avoiding the roadblocks and listening actively. She supports him by the way she listens but does not try to solve his problem and leaves him to deal with it himself. This is a process that will not only help him with his immediate problem but also help him to become a self-directing, responsible adult later in life.

Ben: "Martin has taken my ball away."
Mom: "So Martin took your ball away (paraphrasing) and it looks like you are feeling mad" (reflecting Ben's feelings, i.e., listening actively).
Ben: "Yes, I'm feeling mad, and Martin is no friend of mine if he behaves like that."
Mom: "Mmm" (avoiding bringing anything new to the conversation).
Ben: "Yes, but it's OK, I have other friends."
Mom: "So you feel OK because Martin is not your only friend" (reflecting Ben's feelings and paraphrasing).
Ben: "Yes, and you know what, I don't like what he did, but maybe we can talk about it and maybe he can still be my friend" (Ben finds his own solution).

Example 2

Listening with roadblocks
In this example, see how a common response that is intended to be helpful closes the door to communication.

Liz: (looking worried) "My exam didn't go well."
Mom: "Oh don't worry, I am sure you'll do better next time" (reassuring but disregarding Liz's feelings).
Now Liz doesn't say any more.

Listening actively
In this example, notice how active listening reveals that there is a hidden problem of which the mother was not aware, that Liz has a tricky relationship with her friend Jenny and is worried about what Jenny might say.

Liz: (looking worried) "I didn't do well on my exam."
Mom: "You did badly and aren't happy about it."
Liz: "It's awful, now I won't be able to join the others after school on Friday. Mr. T will make me stay in to catch up."
Mom: "I see, you're disappointed because you'll be missing out. I can understand that."
Liz: "No, it's not that, I promised Jenny I would go out with her and now she is going to be angry with me."
Mom: "Jenny gets upset when you can't go out with her."
Liz: "Oh, she always gets mad when things don't go her way. Sometimes I don't like her because of that."

Example 3

Listening with roadblocks

Clara: "I don't see how I can do this."
Mom: "Of course you can do it!"
Clara: "No, I can't, it will take ages and I don't have time" (resisting).

Listening actively

Clara: "I don't see how I can do this."
Mom: "Sounds like it is quite complicated to do it" (listening actively).
Clara: "It's not complicated, but I have quite a lot on" (no resistance).
Mom: "Ah, I see, you're very busy" (referring to the problem, paraphrasing).

Clara: "Yes, but maybe I could do it in stages. What do you think?" (searching for a solution).

Mom: "Well, if that would work for you that sounds good."

Example 4

Notice that helpful listening happens when we listen to what the speaker is saying. Unhelpful listening happens when we are more interested in telling the other person what we think.

Daniel has a school test tomorrow but wants to play with his friends.

Your possible responses:

1. "How well will you do if you don't prepare for the test tonight?"
2. "How about you prepare for the test and then go and play?"
3. "Well, I don't see how you can play with your friends and prepare properly for the test."
4. "It looks like you are torn between preparing for the test and playing with your friends."

Comments on those possible responses:

1. You ask a question — not letting Daniel find his own solution.
2. You give advice — not letting Daniel find his own solution.
3. You express your opinion — this may shut down communication.

4. You give an active listening response, which is helpful to Daniel. As a result, he will probably talk with you about the problem and may come up with his own solution.

IS THE PROBLEM YOUR PROBLEM OR YOUR CHILD'S PROBLEM?

Many parents take responsibility for their children's problems and try to solve them — and many children think, therefore, that their problems *are* their parents' problem! When parents take on their children's problems, they can feel overburdened and frustrated, while at the same time their children do not learn to take responsibility and resolve their problems for themselves and may even learn to blame others for them.

A problem is the parents' problem if it is something that affects them in a tangible way — for example, if their children make so much noise that they can't concentrate, or if their children have not taken the family pet for a walk despite an agreement to do so. In this case, when a problem is the parent's problem, parents need to use Skill 5 (being assertive) to resolve it.

On the other hand, children own the problem if, for example, they are upset because they lose a ball and can't find it or if they have not been chosen for a school sports team. These are the kinds of problems — frustrations, disappointments, failures, concerns — that children will inevitably face as they go through life, and it is both appropriate and helpful to them that they learn to deal with these problems themselves.

It is important that parents recognize that their children own these kinds of problems and let them take responsibility for them yet remain concerned and willing to help in ways that allow their children to find their own answers. In these circumstances it is invaluable to listen actively and leave children to solve the problem although, of course, they can nevertheless ask their parents to help them if necessary. In this way, they can express their feelings, receive emotional support, calm down, learn to handle their problems, and become self-reliant and self-directing.

> "Never help a child with a task at which he feels he can succeed."
>
> **Maria Montessori**

THE BENEFITS OF ACTIVE LISTENING

Virginia Axline, a former doctoral student of Carl Rogers, was the creator of "Play Therapy," which she based on active listening. In active listening the focus is on the child, not on the child's problem, and by our focusing on the child, the child becomes empowered to find their own solutions. This becomes clear in Axline's wonderful book *Dibs: In Search of Self*, about a severely maltreated boy who recovered and learned to be self-directing and responsible in weekly sessions of play therapy, during which Axline did nothing more than listen actively to him over the course of a year.

If parents listen actively to their children and children develop the habit of sharing their thoughts and feelings with their parents when they are young, they are likely to do so when they are older, when conversations about more difficult topics arise. Being able to talk to their parents about issues such as drugs, or relationships, and knowing that their parents will listen to them and not respond by giving unsolicited advice, can be especially helpful to them.

> "More than IQ, your emotional awareness and ability to handle feelings will determine your success and happiness in all walks of life."
>
> **John Gottman**
> *Raising an Emotionally Intelligent Child*

Listening actively to children when they are young gives them an invaluable basis for acquiring a rich emotional vocabulary and becoming emotionally self-aware so that as they grow older, they are better able to express and communicate their feelings with those around them.

When we paraphrase and reflect, the person being listened to has the opportunity to tell us if we have understood correctly or not. They could say, for example, "Yes, that's right," or "No, I'm not sad, I'm angry" and, as a result, we get to understand their situation better and are likely to see their point of view more easily, feel closer, and have warmer feelings towards them. We are also unlikely to jump to erroneous conclusions.

If your children are now older and you have not practiced listening to them actively, it is never too late. If you start now, it will be more challenging than starting when they were younger, but it can certainly be done. Try to do it a little at a time, in such a way that your children don't notice that you are doing something new. For example, if your child has a problem and says something about it, stop yourself from commenting or giving unsolicited advice. Just say something like "I see, Jim, you are feeling annoyed because they didn't choose you for the team." Then wait to see the response, and if there is one, use the approach again. It will take some time to change habits, and you may find it helpful to find a counselor to support you as you make the changes.

At the same time, when children are listened to, they learn to be good listeners themselves. Every time we practice active listening with children, we are teaching them little by little how to be good listeners themselves.

Active listening promotes good mental health. Children who are listened to actively are likely to talk about their feelings, which is often more helpful than thinking about them. Sometimes when you listen, nothing much seems to happen — and then later you realize that the problem has gone away.

Often when a child starts to talk about their feelings, the original topics turn out to be the tip of the iceberg, and further issues and feelings come to the surface. This makes active listening doubly helpful because, without it, some things may never get to be expressed and dealt with. Later in life, when children who have been listened to become parents, they will be able to listen skillfully to their own children.

Thomas Gordon, also a former doctoral student of Carl Rogers, extended the practice of active listening in therapy sessions to parents in the home and people in the workplace. He recounted the experience of a father who one day truly listened to his 15-year-old daughter for the first time.

Here is what that father said:

> "I learned more about my daughter and what she is like in those 2 hours than I had in the past 5 years. On top of that, the rest of the week she was downright friendly to me. What a change!"
>
> ***Parent Effectiveness Training (P.E.T.)***
> Plume, Penguin, 1970 (page 57)

Listening, paraphrasing and reflecting may seem artificial or counterintuitive at first, but with practice it will become second nature and you will ask yourself how you managed before without it. Active listening will enable you to develop far more satisfying and warmer relationships with your children and with other people, and it will enable your children to do the same. Many adults have never been listened to in this way themselves and it can be a very special experience.

> "I have learned to listen more."
>
> **Girl, 9 years old**
>
> *From video at the end of Cool is Best workshops*

DEMOCRATIC DECISION MAKING: WHY IT IS SO IMPORTANT

Parents will have far better relationships with their children and others if they listen and come to consensual agreements about contentious issues. Being an authoritarian parent may bring quick solutions in the parents' favor, but later, when the children are older and bigger, it will foment rebellion or submission, both equally undesirable. Nor should parents go to the other extreme and be permissive, because then children will come to feel entitled to have their own way. When parents respect and listen to their children they can explain why something bothers them and reach an agreement with their children that resolves the problem. In order for this to work well, it is also important that parents are consistent.

THE ESSENTIAL CONDITIONS FOR LISTENING ACTIVELY

The essential conditions for being able to listen actively are:

1. It is important to make sure that we are thinking in a COOL way, that is, rationally and calmly (see Skill 1), so that we feel emotionally stable while listening to children, or others, talking about a problem.

2. We really want to listen and can listen without distractions.
3. We are able to listen with UPR (unconditional positive regard) and empathy.
4. We really want to be of help so that the other person can express their feelings and find their own way to resolve their problem themselves.
5. We are able to see the person as a separate person and let them be who they are.
6. We can put aside our own feelings about what we are being told and be willing to hear the person's feelings, however strong they may be.
7. We do not use the roadblocks referred to earlier.
8. When there comes a point in the conversation when the person stops talking, we respect that and let the conversation come to an end.
9. We focus on the person and their feelings and not on the problem.

LEARNING TO LISTEN ACTIVELY TOGETHER WITH A FRIEND

Explain to a friend what active listening is and try doing it together. Decide which one of you will talk and which one will listen.

One of you tells the other about some problem. At first, choose a small problem. Speak normally and not too fast. From time to time, the listener paraphrases what is said in their own words and reflects back what they understand to be the speaker's feelings. For example, "I see, Marta was late, and you felt anxious that something might have happened to her."

When you have finished, discuss how you both felt about the process. What did you find easy and what did you find difficult about it? If it seems rather artificial at first — which is likely the first few times you practice this new skill — do not let that stop you from continuing. With practice it becomes quite natural and both of you will appreciate it more and more.

Now change roles.

When you have finished, discuss again how you both felt about the process. Did the speaker like the feeling of being listened to with the full attention of the other person? Did the listener get to better understand the point of view and feelings of the person speaking? Did you see how, if the listener misunderstood something, the speaker had the opportunity to correct you?

After practicing with a friend, you can practice with other people and, even when you go shopping, paraphrase what people say and reflect back how you think they feel! When you are ready, try it out with your children. When they refer to some problem or difficulty they may have, paraphrase what they say in your own words and reflect back what you think is their main feeling. It is important that you paraphrase using your own words and that your response has the feel of a normal conversation as much as possible, and that you show interest in how the other person feels.

Don't expect to be perfect straight away but be committed to working at it. Remember, it is a skill that you can learn!

"This workshop helped me to put empathy into practice and be able to understand my classmates better, in school and outside. I can put myself in another person's place and pay attention to situations that arise and feel myself able to help."

Girl, 13 years old

From video at the end of Cool is Best workshops

COMMON MISTAKES WHEN BEGINNING TO LISTEN ACTIVELY

1. Parroting instead of paraphrasing in one's own words. If we use our own words, the speaker will have the sense that they are being listened to by someone who is interested and listening rather than by someone who is repeating word for word what they are saying.
2. Using a roadblock at some point. If that happens, find a way to take it back and continue listening actively again.
3. Listening at a time when others do not want to talk about their feelings.
4. Not being aware of the person's mood and not stopping when they are no longer interested in talking.

BEING EMPATHIC IF SOMEONE TELLS YOU SOMETHING SHOCKING

In order to be empathic, Carl Rogers says, we must "lay aside our own views and values in order to enter another's world without prejudice."

If we succeed in doing this, it is impossible to be judgmental about other people's actions. If we ask ourselves where the other person has come from or what forces have shaped who they are, put ourselves in their place or imagine we were shaped by the same forces, we will be able to empathize even with someone who has done something terrible, and, by doing so, be of help to that person.

ACTIVITIES TO DO TOGETHER WITH YOUR CHILDREN

PARENT GUIDE: SKILL 4

LISTENING WITH EMPATHY

INTRODUCTION

These activities should be adapted to the ages of the children participating and to your own parental circumstances.

If you find the Six Skills of value you can download the Cool is Best app, where you will find additional resources including videos, audios, and interactive e-books for children from 8 to 14 years old.

Note for teachers: these activities are used successfully in Cool is Best workshops with students in school.

INDEX (40 MINS)

1. Objectives, usefulness, materials
2. Brief review of previous workshops (5 mins)
3. Activity (20 mins)
4. Reflections (5 mins)
5. What have we learned today? The usefulness of the skill (5 mins)
6. Conscious breathing (5 mins)
7. What to do between sessions

1a. OBJECTIVES

- Learning the characteristics of listening with roadblocks
- Learning how to listen with attention
- Learning how to listen with empathy

1b. USEFULNESS OF THE SKILL

- Listening with empathy helps me in my relationships.
- Others appreciate me if I listen to them, accept and value them, and they are therefore more likely to have a good relationship with me.
- I feel good if I can help someone who has a problem by listening to them.

1c. MATERIALS

- Missions for role plays
- Form for observers
- Ball for reflections
- Marker for the board

2. REVIEW OF PREVIOUS SKILLS

We pass the ball and the person who has the ball speaks if they wish.

Skill 1 – Managing my emotions by thinking COOL
Have we been aware of our thinking, of our HOT thoughts and COOL thoughts? And of how we felt? Have we put into practice changing our thoughts from HOT to COOL?

Skill 2 – Recognizing our emotions
Have we been more aware of our emotions, and can we give examples?

Skill 3 – Having healthy self-esteem
Are we accepting ourselves more and feeling better about ourselves?

Conscious breathing
Have we practiced? How did it go?

3. ACTIVITY: ROLE-PLAYS

Let's do some theater!
We explain that there are three ways to listen:
1. Listening with roadblocks
2. Listening with attention
3. Listening with empathy

The parent invites different volunteers to act in the different roles. During the role-playing, one person speaks, one person listens, and the others observe. The person who speaks talks about something they are interested in.

The listener is given a "mission," which instructs them on what kind of listening to use in the role-play. The mission can be hand-written or printed.

Missions for role-plays:

1. Listening with roadblocks

You give a lot of advice You are critical and judgmental. For example: "Well, that wasn't very bright of you."	You avoid eye contact You interrupt a lot	You don't pay attention You say things like: "Well, I wouldn't have done that."

2. Listening with attention

Your posture shows interest	You say things like: "Tell me more." "Mmm." "Ah, I see."	You look the other person in the eye. You move or nod your head to show that you are listening.

3. Listening with empathy

You say things like: "Let me see if I understand."	You say things like: "Ah, so they criticized you unfairly and you were angry."	You say things like: "Ah, so____ happened and you felt____(angry, sad, disappointed, etc.)."

Those who do not play a part in the role-play act as observers. They observe the role-play and try to identify the kind of listening the listener uses and how the speaker feels. They fill in the observer's form as they watch.

OBSERVER'S FORM

Put ticks in the columns according to what you see

3 ways to listen

The person who is listening…	**1** Without attention	**2** With attention	**3** With empathy
Interrupts?			
Is judgmental?			
Gives advice without being asked for it?			
Talks about their own experiences?			
Pays attention?			
Looks in the speaker's eyes?			
Has a posture showing interest?			
Says things like "mmm" (to show they are listening)?			
Nods their head to show they are listening?			
Says things like "I understand...you feel..." ?			
The person who is speaking…			
Feels comfortable?			
Feels listened to?			
Feels understood?			
Feels validated?			

FIRST ROLE-PLAY: LISTENING WITH ROADBLOCKS

Write the missions on paper, fold and put in a bowl, and have everyone take one.

A parent or child talks for approximately one minute about something that interests them or an everyday experience that has happened to them.

Mission for the listener:

- Interrupt a lot or avoid eye contact, and so on.

Note: This can be a lot of fun but in order to avoid the speaker taking the role-play personally, ensure that they understand that they will not be listened to the way they would like. This is especially important for younger children.

The observers fill in the Observers Form.

When the role-play is finished, ask:

- The observers: What have you noticed about the way the listener listened?
- The speaker: How did you feel? Did you feel listened to? Did the way the listener listened to you help you?
- The listener: How did you feel?

As comments are made, parents or children can write them down on a board (or large sheet of paper) under the heading "LISTENING WITH ROADBLOCKS" written at the top on the left side:

LISTENING WITH ROADBLOCKS

SECOND ROLE-PLAY: LISTENING WITH ATTENTION

The speaker
The speaker talks about something that interests them or something that has happened to them.

Mission for the listener:

- Have an attentive posture
- Show interest
- Do not interrupt
- Do not judge or criticize
- Do not give advice
- Look into the speaker's eyes
- Move head from time to time to show that you are listening

The observers fill in the Observers Form
At the end, ask:

- The observers: What did you notice about the way the listener listened?
- The speaker: How did you feel? Did you feel listened to? Did the way the listener listened to you help you?
- The listener: How did you feel?

As comments are made, the parents or children write them down under a second heading: LISTENING WITH ATTENTION (written to the right of the previous heading):

LISTENING WITH ROADBLOCKS	LISTENING WITH WITH ATTENTION

THIRD ROLE PLAY: LISTENING WITH EMPATHY

The speaker

The speaker talks about not just something that interests them but about a problem they have had recently (avoid talking about problems that cause strong emotions).

Mission for the listener:

- The listener listens with empathy, saying things like: "Oh, I understand, I can see it's a problem" or "I understand how you feel."

The listener can also say from time to time:

"I can see that you felt ____________" (how the listener thinks the speaker feels, for example, angry, sad, disappointed).

This kind of comment gives the speaker the chance to confirm that they do feel angry, or that they don't feel angry but sad, for example. This way the listener will know better how the person with the problem really feels.

It is important for the person listening to be sincere when making their comments.

At the end, ask:

- The observers: What did you notice about the way the listener listened?
- The speaker: How did you feel? Did you feel listened to? Did the way you were listened to help you?
- The listener: How did you feel?

As comments are made, the parents or children write them down under a third heading:

"LISTENING WITH EMPATHY," which is added on the far-right side:

LISTENING WITH ROADBLOCKS	LISTENING WITH ATTENTION	LISTENING WITH EMPATHY

4. REFLECTIONS

Some questions to ask at the end of the three role-play activities:

- What differences have we observed between the three kinds of listening?
- What happens when we interrupt?
- What happens when we give advice if the person speaking has not asked for advice?
- What can we do so that the person speaking feels good?
- How do we listen usually?
- Could we listen better?
- Can we give examples of situations in which we have not felt heard?

Additional questions:

- How do we feel when another person is interested in how we feel?
- If we show interest in how another person feels, is it likely that we will have a better relationship with them?
- In other words, will listening with empathy help us in our relationships?

5. WHAT HAVE WE LEARNED TODAY?

We can emphasize the two or three most important points:

- What are the differences between listening with roadblocks, with attention and with empathy?
- Is listening with empathy most appropriate when we are listening to someone who has a problem?

On the USEFULNESS of the skill:

- Do we agree that we can help someone solve their problem by listening to them actively and by giving them the space to express how they feel?
- How do you think it helps you if you listen actively? Do you think it will help you in your relationships with other people?

6. CONSCIOUS BREATHING

If you have downloaded the Cool is Best app, you will find an audio recording for Skill 4 that you can listen to if you wish.

Let's sit in a comfortable position with our eyes closed, our backs straight, our shoulders back in an open position and our feet in contact with the ground, without crossing our legs.

We put one hand on our stomach and the other on our chest and we notice that our body is moving, and that it is moving because of our breathing.

We have nothing else to do right now, we just focus our attention on our breathing. We focus our attention on the here and now, in the present moment.

We continue to breathe, each of us at our own pace. We focus our attention on our breathing. If any thought or concern arises, it doesn't matter. When we become aware of it, we simply turn our attention back to our breathing. If we like, we can transform the thought into a bird and let it fly away.

Now, while we continue to breathe, we also put our attention on our feet, and on their contact with the ground. We are going to feel very relaxed and heavy. This sensation goes up our legs, our knees. Our legs feel very relaxed and heavy. This sensation rises up our body, the lower part of the back and the stomach. We feel all these areas very relaxed, and we feel the pleasant sensation that relaxation gives us.

The sensation goes up the chest, the back, the shoulders, it goes down the arms and reaches the hands, which become very relaxed and heavy. It goes up the neck, the head, and reaches the eyes, the eyelids and the lips. We feel our whole body very relaxed and heavy. We continue to breathe, and we feel like our whole body is breathing.

Now let's think of someone we care about. We are going to visualize that person and we are going to wish them great happiness. **Let's imagine how we would listen to them when they explain something to us.** Let's imagine that they explain a problem they have and how we respond by saying, "Yes, I can see that is a problem," and how we see that the other person feels a sense of relief because they have been listened to, heard, and validated.

Now we do the same thing with someone with whom we have a problem. Let's take a moment to see that person. **Let's imagine how we would listen to them** when they explain the problem from their point of view, and how we respond by saying, "Yes, I can see that is a problem for you," and how we see that the other person feels a sense of relief because they have been listened to, heard and validated.

Brief pause.

We continue to breathe, paying attention to our breathing. We take a deep breath, calmly and without exaggeration. A second breath. And a third. And little by little we move our toes, our bodies, our fingers, and we open our eyes.

After pausing a moment, we can talk about how the conscious breathing went. How did we feel? What did we notice?

Have we practiced during the week?

If some of us have difficulties, we can talk about them and remind ourselves that conscious breathing, like any skill, gets easier with practice.

We can recommend finding a time of day during the week (it is better if it is always the same time) to practice.

7. WHAT TO DO BETWEEN SESSIONS

The parent can ask if anyone would like to make any comments and then suggest that we practice conscious breathing and listening with both attention and empathy during the following week.

HOW DID THE ACTIVITIES GO?

Maybe they went really well, and you are happy with how they went.

Or maybe you didn't find it so easy. If that was the case, don't be discouraged! These things can take time. And, of course, a lot depends on the ages of your children and your own emotional situation. So just focus on the fact that practicing Skill 4 is of enormous benefit for you and your children, now and in the future, and find a way that works for you to put it into practice.

In order to keep Skills 1, 2, 3 and 4 in mind, do the conscious breathing activity regularly and incorporate visualizations of the four skills.

QUESTIONNAIRE SKILL 4

KEY:
4-Totally Agree
3-Agree
2-Disagree
1-Totally Disagree

NOTE: Put a circle around the number of your reply.

a. Now I can see that I can help other people who have problems if I listen to them with empathy.
1— 2 — 3 — 4

b. Now I see that listening to other people with empathy helps me to establish good relationships with them.
1— 2 — 3 — 4

c. I would recommend this skill to my friends.
1— 2 — 3 — 4

SKILL 5

COMMUNICATING ASSERTIVELY
Being Able to Resolve Conflicts in a Way That Satisfies Everyone (Win-Win)

When we communicate assertively — rather than aggressively or passively — we take into account other people's needs, desires and feelings as well as our own and help to resolve problems and conflicts in a way that satisfies everyone. As a result, people feel good about each other and if family members are involved, they will be unlikely to estrange later in life.

There are three principal ways of communicating

- Aggressively
- Passively
- Assertively

The way people communicate depends on the circumstances. We may be passive when the issues are minor but assertive when the stakes are higher. A person may be aggressive with certain people but passive with others. Nevertheless, we each tend to have a predominant style, and this has an important effect on our relationships.

At one extreme is **aggressive communication** — we defend and insist on our rights, needs and desires but do not respect other people's rights, needs or desires. We talk, but do not let or encourage others to talk.

At the other extreme is **passive, or avoidant, communication** — we don't speak up to defend our rights and interests and we allow other people to ignore them.

The third style is **assertive communication** — we communicate reasonably and rationally, we stand up for ourselves and defend our interests, but we also respect the interests of others. Ideally, we are also skilled at listening (Skill 4).

Aggressive communication

A common misconception is that aggressiveness means being violent physically, but a person can be aggressive in a seemingly polite way without even raising their voice.

People who communicate aggressively:

- Do not have healthy self-esteem
- Defend and insist on their rights, needs and desires but do not respect other people's rights, needs or desires
- Do not recognize or take into account what other people think, want or need
- Express their ideas, opinions and desires in a way that disregards others and often hurts them
- Act with a complete lack of empathy
- Become upset (angry, depressed, insecure) when others do not do what they want
- Blame and put down others in order to dominate them and make them feel bad

As a result, people become resentful and even fearful, and either pander to them or avoid them if they can.

Acting aggressively has a lot to do with a lack of self-esteem: If I don't feel good about myself, I may try to compensate by being aggressive, whereas a person with healthy self-esteem respects both themself and others.

People who communicate aggressively *think* (without necessarily being aware of it):

- I *have to* get what I want
- If I don't win it means that I lose

- My opinions are facts. Facts that contradict my opinions are not facts and have no value
- What I think and want is more important than what other people think and want
- Other people should do what I want

And they *feel*:
- Powerful when others comply
- Angry when others do not comply
- Vulnerable lest they lose their power

Passive communication
This is the opposite of aggressive communication.

People who communicate passively:
- Also do not have healthy self-esteem
- Accept that the rights, needs, desires, and opinions of others are more important than their own
- Leave others to make decisions
- Do not succeed in having their opinions considered
- Can be taken advantage of and have their desires and rights ignored
- May agree to something even though they are against it
- Can become spectators of life as it passes them by
- Blame other people for their problems

People who communicate passively *think* (without necessarily being aware of it) that:
- What other people think and want is more important than what I think and want or need

- I would do better to keep quiet because I will not get the outcomes I want, and making a fuss might get me into a worse situation.
- Speaking up would be a scary prospect

And they can *feel*:

- Frustrated, impotent, depressed, angry, resentful or worthless — often without being fully aware of it

Assertive communication

The third style is assertive communication — we communicate reasonably and rationally, and we stand up for ourselves and defend our interests, but we also respect the interests and feelings of others.

People who communicate assertively:

- Have healthy self-esteem and no hidden agenda
- Respect themselves and stand up for themselves, their rights, needs and desires, but they also listen to others and respect their rights, needs and desires (Skill 4)
- Are likely to get the things that they want and have personal satisfaction in their lives
- Choose to think COOL (Skill 1) and have thoughts that are free of:
    -Exaggeration, demandingness, and put-downs
    -Inability to tolerate frustration
    -Jumping to wrong conclusions, blaming, criticizing, judging, taking things personally

- Are in control of their emotions and have healthy feelings about themselves and about others (Skill 3)
- Are empathic (Skill 4)
- Let others know what they think, feel, want and need in a calm, transparent way without any kind of manipulation (Skill 1)
- Have no problem apologizing for their mistakes
- Look for solutions acceptable to everyone when problems or conflicts arise (note: it is better, if possible, not to address problems by email because it is easy to misinterpret what someone writes and jump to wrong conclusions)
- Have good relations with most people
- Say yes if they want to say yes, and no if they want to say no
- Ask for an explanation if they don't understand something
- Have a relaxed posture, and make appropriate expressions and gestures with their face and hands
- What they say and how they say it is congruent with their body language; they talk in a steady, warm way, at a normal volume and look other people in the eye

"Assertiveness helps us to be able to accept the opinion of others and not shut ourselves in on only our own opinions but understand everyone's point of view, and know that by combining ideas we can create something better."

Girl, 13 years old

From video at the end of Cool is Best workshops

Family relationships and democratic decision making

Many parents treat their children in an authoritarian way and may obtain certain benefits from this while their children are young. But later, when the children are older and bigger, a power struggle begins in which the children resist the domination of their parents. To avoid this and the bad feelings it causes, and the possible future estrangement that may result, we should treat children with respect from an early age and always listen to them and take their views into account. If we do this, we lessen or avoid the rebellion of adolescence, and we model for children how to be assertive adults in the future.

Sharing family decisions is not always easy and there are times when we may be unsure what to do, but if we are persistent and think COOL and are empathic, we can always find solutions that satisfy everyone. It takes more time at first but, after we have been putting it into practice for a while, problems are likely to be resolved quickly.

Ineffective communication — You-messages

If you want to say something nice to your children such as "You look as if you are really enjoying that!" a You-message is perfectly appropriate.

But using You-messages in the following ways is counterproductive:

"You must not do that" (commanding)

"You ought to know better" (putting down)

"It's your fault" (blaming)

These You-messages damage relationships because ordering, putting down, judging, blaming convey the message that there is something wrong with the person or that they are inferior in some way. You-messages undermine a child's sense of self-acceptance, block cooperation, breed resistance and resentment and may lead to retaliation.

How would you respond if someone gave you this You-message: "You said you would arrive on time. Why didn't you call to say that you would be late?" Note that in this example, the speaker has not taken into account the possibility that you wanted to call but that you weren't able to.

Yet these are the kinds of You-messages that parents often say to their children.

Effective communication — I-messages

When children cause us a problem, the most effective way of addressing it is to use an I-message. It is important to do this in a calm and respectful way and at a moment in which everyone concerned is emotionally calm. This is a skill that is essential for both parents and children to learn because it is an effective way to resolve conflicts.

The I-message has three parts:

1. Describe or refer to the situation or behavior that is causing the problem, as you see it. It is important to be specific and accurate and stick to observable facts. For example, you might say, "We agreed that the kitchen floor would be kept clear so that I can get our meal ready, but there are things all over the floor." Note that this is simply a statement of fact and conveys no judgment. It is important to make sure that your speaking tone and body language are equally nonjudgmental.

2. Say how this affects you tangibly and concretely: "With things all over the floor, I can't cook." When you explain this, your children will be able to understand that there is a problem.

3. Communicate using an I-message by stating how you feel about the situation or behavior that you have described. For example, you might say: "I feel frustrated (I-message) that I can't cook because we're all hungry and will want to eat soon."

An I-message is effective because it is less likely to be seen as threatening by the person to whom it is directed, unlike many You-messages, and it therefore does not cause resistance or defensiveness.

If at any time your children show that they have problems with what you are saying — for example, they may shrug their shoulders — you then change to **listening** mode (Skill 4) and paraphrase and reflect back to them what you understand them to be saying and feeling. Be prepared to do this as often, and for as long, as necessary. By listening in this way, you make it much more likely that your children — or anyone else — will listen to what you have to say and take it into account.

This may not happen straight away, and you may need to practice this with persistence over a period of time, especially if there are resentments caused by inappropriate You-messages in the past.

If you keep an open mind, when you switch to listening (and paraphrasing and reflecting), you may be surprised to hear something from your children that will change the way you think about the problem. You may even decide that there is in fact no problem! As you will discover, this is a common experience.

Switching from using an I-message to listening, and then going back to using another I-message, may not be easy at first because it requires awareness, patience and practice, but it is a skill that can be learned and it will foster good relations in the family. It is never too late to start practicing this skill with your family members.

1. An example of using I-messages:

You: "Tim, we agreed that you would be back at eight o'clock, but you didn't arrive on time, and I was worried" (I-message).

Tim: "Oh come on, you have no need to be worried" (Tim interprets your message as critical, even though it was simply stating a fact).

You: "I see, you think that if you aren't back when you said you would be, I shouldn't worry" (listening actively, Skill 4).

Tim: "Yeah, but I guess I can see your point. I'll call next time if I am going to be late" (Tim no longer feels attacked and suggests a possible solution).

It is also a good idea to preface the three-part I-message with a statement of understanding or empathy. For example, you could say: "Hey guys, I know it can be difficult to clean up when you are having fun." Make sure that you do not follow this with a "but" because the "but" would undermine your statement of understanding. In place of a "but," just pause a second before continuing with the first part of the I-message, which was, "We agreed that the kitchen floor would be kept clear so that I can get our meal ready and there are things all over the floor."

As you give your message — including a possible introductory statement of understanding or empathy — be very aware that being angry, complaining, blaming and so on are ineffective and counterproductive. In order to be successful, prepare yourself with COOL, helpful thinking (Skill 1), possibly doing a visualization before you begin.

You may not need to say any more. You have given whoever left the things on the floor the information they need to do the responsible thing. If you say no more and if at some point your children make themselves busy clearing up, you will have achieved your goal, and given your children the chance to take responsibility for their actions, and created harmony in the home.

2. Try not to suggest a solution to problems; instead, leave the solution to those who caused the problem because

this helps them become conscious of their responsibility. However, if this does not happen, even after you've been trying hard, you can go on to a *fourth step* and say what you would like or expect to happen. For example, you could say, "We agreed that the kitchen floor would be kept clear, and I would like you guys to clear it up."

3. If progress is still not made, you can go on to resolve the conflict using the win-win conflict resolution process discussed later in this chapter.

Identify a situation in which you would like to be more assertive

Identify a situation when you don't feel good because you do not behave assertively and describe it (not vaguely but specifically).

____

____

____

____

____

The account should include the following points:

- *What* happens
- *When* it happens
- *Who* is the person, or the people, involved
- *How* you act in that situation
- *What* you would like to happen instead (your goal)
- The consequences you *fear* if you were to be assertive
- Your goal

For example, this account is *too vague*:

"Other people don't listen to me. When this happens, I feel disregarded. I would like others to listen to me."

Here is an example of an account that works because it is *specific*:

"When I meet Bob and Lakeesha (*who*) after work (*when*), I don't think they value what I have to say (*what*). I therefore often keep quiet (*how I act*). If I were to speak up more, I think they might put me down (*my fear*). I feel insecure because of this and would like them to listen to me and show interest in what I say (*goal*)."

The most important step in order to change this scenario is to change your thoughts and beliefs from "I can't handle this situation" to "Yes, I can handle this situation," and then change your behavior, either progressively or all at once.

Imagine different situations and role-play them

In order to train yourself and your children to be assertive, think of scenes that are difficult and then imagine them with successful outcomes and role-play them.

Example:

"Yesterday (*when*) my teacher Jane (*who*) gave me an unfair mark (*what*). I would normally not say anything and would instead just feel resentful, but this time I want to be assertive and discuss the mark with her (*goal*)."

In order to do this successfully, the first step is to make sure that you are thinking in a COOL way (Skill 1).

Think about what a COOL way of thinking would be

in this situation. Do not expect others to know what you want unless you let them know!

Here are some more examples to practice with:

- You broke something by mistake.
- You have to do a presentation.
- Someone has accused you of doing something you didn't do.
- Another kid is being ignored.
- Someone cuts into a line.

What would your assertive response be in each case?

Saying no

Many adults and children can find it difficult to say no. In order to be able to say no, visualize the scene, decide on the thoughts that will help you achieve your goal and practice them again and again, and you will find that you and your children can learn to say no.

Preventing manipulation and false accusations — always require evidence that is verifiable

It is, unfortunately, common for people to make false accusations. Sometimes the accusations are made out of ignorance, sometimes they are made consciously and maliciously with the intention of causing damage. Some people are very skillful at manipulating. For example, they take an apparently questionable action by the person they want to attack, and they refer to it subtly over time so that others eventually come to say to themselves "Aha, that person is suspect."

Imagine your teenage son is told by a manipulative friend that a third friend has said nasty things about him behind his back. In these circumstances, he needs to be assertive and check the facts with that third friend because if he believes the accusations, which are not true, he can end up losing the wrong friend.

Similarly, your children need to know that it is vital to be assertive in order to avoid falling under the influence or control of a controlling or manipulative partner or sect.

Complete these sentences:

Being assertive means that I

____

____

____

____

____

Some possible endings to this sentence:

I would stand up for myself more.

I would not be afraid of the reactions of others if I spoke up.

I would be respected more and be taken more seriously by others.

If I am not assertive, it means that I

____

____

____

____

If I believed in myself more than I do, I

If I were more assertive, how would I feel about myself?

How would feeling better about myself help me
in other areas of my life?

How can I get to believe in myself more?

The most common but ineffective ways to resolve conflicts

Parents generally use one of two ways to resolve conflicts. Sometimes they fluctuate between the two methods. Both of them involve power struggles and both of them have harmful consequences. Often parents realize this but do not see any alternative.

Win-Lose: Parents win, children lose

Parents who are authoritarian resolve conflicts using their power. They tell their children how things are going to be and often use rewards and punishments to get their children to do what they want. When this happens, parents get their own needs met and do not fully consider their children's needs. But there are serious problems with this very common approach.

To succeed with this approach, parents need to have power over their children, but that power diminishes as children grow older and bigger and capable of being more independent. Although being authoritarian (which, in terms of Skill 1, is to be demanding) can appear to work when children are little, the children are likely to rebel against their parents' authority as they get older. If they do not rebel, they are likely to become submissive. In neither case will the children learn to become self-directing or to form constructive, happy relationships; and in both cases, they are likely to resist, feel resentful and even retaliate. They will hide their feelings and their thoughts. Meanwhile, if children do not submit, the parents are likely to experience strong feelings such as anger and resentment as the power struggle continues and grows over time. As a result, the relationship suffers and **win-lose** becomes **lose-lose.** This dynamic can lead to estrangement later in life.

Lose-Win: Parents lose, children win
Parents who are passive or permissive let their children hold the upper hand to get what they want and do what they like, often at the expense of the parents' own wants, needs and peace of mind. Parents who allow their children to behave in this way are teaching their children that it is OK to be self-centered and selfish. Consequently, these parents may suffer at the hands of their children over the years and come to feel considerable resentment. This can lead them to estrange later if the resentment is strong enough.

Resolving conflicts effectively: Win-win
Being able to resolve problems and conflicts on a win-win basis means that all parties feel happy with the outcome.

This is a much better way of resolving problems and conflicts than the common win-lose or lose-win methods. In win-win, there is no use of power by any of the parties and therefore there is no power struggle. Solutions are not imposed by anyone, and everyone has an equal say in decisions that affect them. A solution is found that satisfies everyone. Problems and conflicts are accepted as something that is natural and inevitable in life, and when they arise emotions are not aroused, at least not for long. Problems are seen as a challenge to be resolved rather than a threat to be avoided at all costs.

Win-win is based on the idea that we can cooperate to find solutions that satisfy all parties and have excellent relationships even when there are problems.

The win-win approach may take a little more time and effort at first, but in the long run it saves a huge amount of time and energy for everyone involved.

Win-win promotes good feelings and cooperation rather than resistance or rebellion because win-win agreements are in everyone's interests. Win-win solutions also motivate everyone involved to do their part to make the solution a success. In the case of parent and child win-win agreements, this is extremely liberating for parents because it frees them from having to supervise, follow up and nag their children.

When parents and children discover that they can work things out in this way, their confidence in themselves grows, as does their trust in the other people involved.

When difficult situations arise, people do not avoid talking about them but are happy to look for solutions to the problem. By involving everybody, there is a greater chance that a satisfactory solution will be found because several people are more likely to come up with a creative solution than just one or two people.

Win-win promotes cooperation and good feelings rather than antagonism. During the process, all parties identify what is important and both children and parents are free to change their minds as a result of listening to each other.

The win-win approach clearly enables parents and children to have better relationships. Finding mutually beneficial solutions prepares kids and parents to get along once kids become teenagers.

Children who have been listened to and involved in win-win problem solving will not want to estrange from their parents or siblings. Parents who have not listened to their children before can change and learn to listen actively (Skill 4) and communicate assertively.

Active listening is an integral part of win-win problem solving and, as we saw in Skill 4, listening actively often helps reveal issues underlying a problem.

After practicing win-win problem solving for some time you will find that the number of conflicts falls dramatically. Children who know that their opinions are taken into account by their parents appreciate the fact that their parents treat them with respect and do not abuse their power. Children who feel heard and valued become more accepting, and conflict reduces.

If you have imposed decisions in the past but now want to change to win-win, your children may be skeptical at first and you will probably find that there will be a process of adjustment.

If your children are already teenagers and have become accustomed to winning at your expense, it will be a challenge for you to introduce win-win. To be successful, you have to believe firmly that you have rights and that it is vital for your children to learn to negotiate as equal partners, and you will again probably find that there will be a process of adjustment. It may be helpful to find a counsellor to help you with this change when you first try it.

An example of win-win

A father is worried that his son gets distracted when he gets home from school and therefore doesn't do his homework. Instead of telling his son that he has to do his homework as soon as he gets home, the conversation goes like this:

Father: I don't feel comfortable if you don't do your homework as soon as you get home from school, because when you do other things first it often doesn't get done (I-message).

Child: But when I come home, I want to relax.
I don't want to do more work!

Father: I understand you feel like having a break. I feel the same when I come home (being empathic). However, I am concerned (I-message), so how about we try to find a solution that satisfies us both?

Child: How about you relax about me doing what I want when I come home from school, and I commit to doing my homework sometime before supper?

Father: OK, sounds good to me.

"The workshops have helped me to be more assertive."

Boy, 9 years old

From video at the end of Cool is Best workshops

Win-win has six steps

1. All parties to a conflict agree to using the win-win process. Then they use I-messages to describe how they see the problem and how it tangibly affects them, so that the conflict is clearly identified.

   An example of a parent's I-message might be: "I feel happier when the kitchen is tidy. When toys are scattered all over the floor and I trip over them, the mess makes me anxious, and I would like us to find a solution to the problem that suits all of us."

An example of a child's I-message to a parent might be: "I don't like it when you put all my things away without asking me and then I can't find them and I get mad."

2. All the parties involved listen actively to the others in order to understand the issue from their point of view. Listening actively to someone will allow that person to feel more comfortable and less defensive because their needs and feelings are being heard and taken into account. Listening actively is especially important if their words or body language suggest discomfort or resistance.

3. Brainstorm for possible solutions and write them down. At this stage, no one comments or makes any kind of judgment on the suggestions.

4. Evaluation of proposals. Once everybody has made their suggestions, all the parties involved evaluate the proposals. The first step is for people to say if there are any proposals that are not acceptable to them and to eliminate them. If a proposal is unacceptable to you, you explain your point of view using an I-message in order to let the other people concerned know what you think and how you feel.

For example, you might say, "I would worry too much if…." Then, if there is a reaction to this, you actively listen to the person until you can see that they feel heard, and that any resistance reduces. Don't move on to the next step too quickly!

Active listening often throws up a suggestion that

resolves the issues in a creative way. For example, if you have a problem because your children aren't polite to your friends when they come around, you may discover through active listening that your children don't want to be rude but do not want to have to spend time with your friends. A mutually satisfactory solution to this problem could be an agreement that when your friends visit, your children say "hi" in an agreeable way and then go off and do something they want to do on their own.

5. Agree on a solution together. Win-win means that everybody cares about the needs of others as well as their own, an approach that greatly strengthens relationships. Therefore, don't try to persuade anyone to accept a particular proposal but rather try to find a solution together that everyone feels happy with and, when it has been agreed on, make a clear agreement together about:

    - *what* each person will do
    - *when* they will do it
    - and *for how long*

    Always honor your agreement. Agree to try the solution out for a time, say, a week, and to amend it together if it doesn't work out. It is a good idea to write the agreement down. If an agreement is not working out, be sure to use I-messages and to use your active listening skills to renegotiate or to remind others of the agreement.

    When a solution has been chosen, one or more of the parties can give a message of appreciation: "I appreciate that we have been able to work together like this and come up with a solution that we all feel comfortable with! If it doesn't work out, of course we will meet again and find a better solution."

6. Put the solution into practice. Results are likely to be good because a mutually chosen agreement is in everyone's interest. However, if others do not do what they have agreed to, do not think in terms of blame and punishment. You want the win-win process to work. If you are doing it with your children you will be helping them to become responsible, self-directing adults, whereas punishment would make them rebellious and resentful or subservient.

   So, for example, if you are in a win-win agreement with your children, and they do not carry out their side of the agreement, give them an I-message such as "I am disappointed that you haven't done what you said you would." Then actively listen to them as they reply. Get to understand the situation from their point of view. If the agreed-upon solution still works for them, find a way together for them to do their part. If it does not suit them, go back to the win-win process and look for alternative solutions. Perhaps the first solution was too difficult for them. One reason for this could be that they have not yet developed sufficient self-directing abilities. If so, you may be able to find a way to help them. For example, if the task has been forgotten, you could give them a note card on which they can write themselves a reminder.

   Review progress periodically to see how the agreement is going and make changes if necessary. Ask everybody, "Are you still happy with the agreement?"

If not, you can modify it together. This review process is important in order to make win-win work well from the beginning and create the confidence to apply it on future occasions. Once the process has been successfully used on several occasions, you will find it easier, and family relations will become more cooperative and less stressful.

When there is a conflict of values

Often parents and children, like adults, have different values. When this happens, ask yourself how important the issue is and if you can live with what your child values. If it doesn't affect you tangibly and concretely, it is best to let your children do what they want. You can do this more easily if you adopt a COOL thought such as, "I would *prefer* that Kenny had shorter hair, but even if he doesn't, it doesn't affect me tangibly and I can think COOL about it and feel OK about it." This approach enables you to avoid having unnecessary arguments and maybe having your children estrange at some later date.

To put this approach into practice, prepare a sheet of paper with two columns. On the left side, write down the things that are really important to you, and on the right side, write those points that you are happy for children to decide for themselves. The fewer items you write on the left side the better!

Treat your children the way you treat your friends

If you treat your children the way you treat your friends, you will never force them to do anything and will always seek win-win solutions. You may seek to influence them, but you will leave decisions with them. If you do this you will remain friends with them as they grow up, whereas if you do not, you will have more difficulties with them than necessary and, when they are older, they may not have the warm feelings towards you that you would like them to have, and they may distance themselves from you.

Child-child conflicts

When two or more children have a problem or conflict, it is vital that they understand and practice the Six Skills in order to be able to work on the problem successfully. In these circumstances, the best thing a parent can do is to keep out of the conflict and let the children resolve it themselves.

If children do not yet have the Six Skills, and cannot do this, you can help by actively listening to them in order to help them calm their feelings, and you can then help them find a win-win solution together.

Be a good model because children imitate their parents!

If you want your children to practice the Six Skills and adopt your values, you only have to be a good model. Children will notice if you do as you say, and this will play a large role in whether they learn to practice the Six Skills and whether they adopt or reject your values.

ACTIVITIES TO DO TOGETHER WITH YOUR CHILDREN

PARENT GUIDE: SKILL 5

BEING ASSERTIVE INSTEAD OF AGGRESSIVE OR PASSIVE

INTRODUCTION

These activities should be adapted to the ages of the children participating and to your own parental circumstances.

If you find the Six Skills of value, you can download the Cool is Best app, where you will find additional resources including videos, audios, and interactive e-books for children from 8 to 14 years old.

Note for teachers: these activities are used successfully in Cool is Best workshops with students in school.

INDEX (40 MINS)

1. Objectives, usefulness, materials
2. Brief review of previous workshops (5 mins)
3. Activity (20 mins)
4. Reflections (5 mins)
5. What have we learned today? The usefulness of the skill (5 mins)
6. Conscious breathing (5 mins)
7. What to do between sessions

1a. OBJECTIVES

- Knowing the three communication styles: assertive, aggressive and passive.
- Understanding the benefits of being assertive, even with people who communicate or act aggressively.
- Seeing that being assertive enables everyone to win (win-win), rather than some win and others lose (win-lose) or some lose and others win (lose-win).
- Understanding the consequences of each communication style.
- Seeing that we do not necessarily always communicate with the same style, but that it can depend on the situation and the people with whom we relate.

1b. USEFULNESS OF THE SKILL

Adopting an assertive communication style helps me to:

- Feel better about myself.
- Have better relationships with others.
- Achieve my goals with more certainty.
- Resolve problems and conflicts.

1c. MATERIALS

- Form for observers: to note how the actors communicate during the role-playing
- Document: The Three Styles of Communication
- Marker for the board
- Ball for reflections

2. REVIEW OF PREVIOUS SKILLS

We pass the ball and the person who has the ball speaks if they wish.

Skill 1 – Managing my emotions by thinking COOL
Have we been aware of our thinking, of our HOT thoughts and COOL thoughts? And of how we have felt? Have we put into practice changing our HOT thoughts to COOL?

Skill 2 – Recognizing my emotions
Have we been more aware of our emotions, and can we give examples?

Skill 3 – Healthy self-esteem
Are we accepting ourselves more and feeling better about ourselves?

Skill 4 – Listening with empathy
Have we been listening with empathy?

Conscious breathing.
Have we practiced? How did it go?

3. ACTIVITY: ROLE-PLAYING

The activity consists of three role-playing activities, followed by reflecting together on what has been learned about the different styles of communication.

THE THREE STYLES OF COMMUNICATION

AGGRESSIVE	PASSIVE	ASSERTIVE
You are only interested in what you need or want. It doesn't matter to you what others need or want. You don't take the feelings of others into account. You put others down. You can be violent. Note: you can communicate aggressively without being violent. You don't respect boundaries	You don't say — or defend — what you need or want. You say yes to things you do not agree with. You don't say no to things you disagree with.	You take into account your own needs and the desires and needs of others. You take into account your own feelings and those of others. You try to find solutions that are a win-win for all concerned.

Volunteers act in the role-play and the others watch and note their observations on the "observer's form."

OBSERVERS' FORM

SKILL 5: ASSERTIVE COMMUNICATION

	Characters in the role-play				
Write Yes or No in the different columns according to what you have observed	1	2	3	4	5
Takes into account the wishes of the others					
Has a flexible point of view					
Defends his/her point of view assertively					
Helps find a win-win solution					
Comment separately on anything else you find of interest.					

Role-play 1

Situation: Five friends (you can adapt this for fewer people) are going on a special trip and want to decide where they are going.

Friend 1: wants to go on a trip to Italy because of pizza and partying. This friend is to act using the aggressive style.

Friend 2: wants to go to London to practice English. This friend is also to act using aggressive style.

Friend 3: would like to go to London, but tries to reach an agreement that satisfies everyone. This friend acts in the assertive style.

Friend 4: has the same opinion as Friend 1 and simply defends his friend's opinion. This friend acts in the passive style.

Friend 5: wants to go to Paris to visit their grandparents. This friend is to act using the aggressive style.

At the end of the role-play:

Ask the observers, actors and listeners what they noticed about the different ways of communicating:

- How did we feel when we watched the aggressive communication style — or played it?
- How did we feel when we watched the passive communication style — or played it?
- How did we feel when we watched the assertive communication style — or played it?

We also ask: What style of communication do we ourselves normally use?

Do we always use the same style, or does it depend on the situation and on who is involved?

Would we be better off if we always communicated assertively?

We then ask all the actors to adopt an assertive style and to find a solution to the problem that is satisfactory to all ("win-win").

Finally we ask the actors to do the role play again with all of them adopting the assertive style and trying to find a win-win solution to the problem.

Role-play 2
A family is having a meal.

Mother: will not let her daughter go to a birthday party on Saturday under any circumstances. She acts using the aggressive style.
Father: if it were up to him, he would let her go. But he uses the passive style and leaves the outcome to the others.

Daughter 1: insists on going to the birthday party. She uses the aggressive style.
Daughter 2: tries to get mother and daughter to reach an agreement. She uses the assertive style.

At the end of the role-play, we ask the same questions as at the end of the previous role-play.

Now, we ask all the actors to adopt an assertive style and to look for a solution that is satisfactory to all ("win-win").

Role-play 3
Three friends are deciding how to spend the evening.

Friend 1: wants to go to a movie and eat popcorn. She is to act using the aggressive style.
Friend 2: doesn't like the movie and wants to go out for a meal. She is to act passively.
Friend 3: acts assertively, and suggests they go to the movie and then have a meal (a possible win-win solution).

At the end of the role-play, ask the same questions as at the end of the previous role-plays.

Then, we suggest that all the actors adopt an assertive style and try to find a "win-win" solution satisfactory to all.

4. REFLECTIONS

- Do we have a different communication style with different people?
- What communication style works best?
- In what situations is it easier for us to be assertive?
- And in what situations is it more difficult?
- How do other people usually communicate with us?
- Is it always beneficial to be assertive?
- Does it help us to consider what others want and what they feel?
- Does being assertive help us to be better at solving problems and conflicts?
- Does being assertive help us to have better relationships and also to achieve our goals?
- What if we are too assertive? Would that be close to being aggressive?
- Is it necessary to be physically violent to be aggressive?
- Is it easier to be assertive if we think COOL and if we have healthy self-esteem?

Clarify:

- We do not necessarily always have the same style of communication with everyone and in all circumstances.
- Although we can strive to give the best of ourselves

by being more assertive, there are people who will continue to adopt an unsatisfactory communication style when they relate to us.

- There will always be problems and conflicts in our lives and what is important is how we resolve them.
- It is very helpful to think that the difficulties that arise in my life are a great opportunity to practice my skills!
- Difficult people are our best teachers because they give us practice so that we become more skilled.

5. WHAT HAVE WE LEARNED TODAY?

Emphasize the most important points:

- To be assertive means that we take into account the needs and desires not only of ourselves but also of others.
- There are three communication styles: aggressive, passive and assertive.
- We do not necessarily have a single communication style; it will depend on the people and the situation in which we find ourselves.
- Being assertive helps us to improve our relationships (with family, friends, colleagues, etc.).

6. CONSCIOUS BREATHING

If you have downloaded the Cool is Best app you will find an audio recording for Skill 5 that you can listen to if you wish.

Let's sit in a comfortable position with our eyes closed, our backs straight, our shoulders back in an open position and our feet in contact with the ground, without crossing our legs.

We put one hand on our stomach and the other on our chest and we notice that our body is moving, and that it is moving because of our breathing.

We have nothing else to do right now, we just focus our attention on our breathing. We focus our attention on the here and now, in the present moment.

We continue to breathe, each of us at our own pace. We focus our attention on our breathing. If any thought or concern arises, it doesn't matter. When we become aware of it, we simply turn our attention back to our breathing. If we like, we can transform the thought into a bird and let it fly away.

Now, while we continue to breathe, we also put our attention on our feet, and on their contact with the ground. We are going to feel very relaxed and heavy. This sensation goes up our legs, our knees. Our legs feel very relaxed and heavy. This sensation rises up our body, the lower part of the back and the stomach. We feel all these areas very relaxed, and we feel the pleasant sensation that relaxation gives us.

The sensation goes up the chest, the back, the shoulders. It goes down the arms and reaches the hands, which become very relaxed and heavy. It goes up the neck, the head, and reaches the eyes, the eyelids and the lips. We feel our whole body very relaxed and heavy. We continue to breathe, and we feel like our whole body is breathing.

Brief pause.

Now let's think of someone with whom we have a problem. We visualize that person and how we talk with them in an assertive way, taking into account their needs and wishes as much as our own. This is not easy at first.

But we use all our skills, and we persist. It doesn't matter that the other person does not have the same skills; our skills cause them to relax more than before, and we are able to dialogue with them. And we see how the problem is resolved in a way that satisfies both of us. Win-win!

Brief pause.

We continue to breathe, paying attention to our breathing. We take a deep breath, calmly and without exaggeration. A second breath. And a third. And little by little we move our toes, our bodies, our fingers, and we open our eyes.

After pausing a moment, we can talk about how the conscious breathing went. How did we feel? What did we notice?

Have we practiced during the week?

If some of us have difficulties, we can talk about them and remind ourselves that conscious breathing, like any skill, gets easier with practice.

We can recommend finding a time of day during the week (it is better if it is always the same time) to practice.

7. WHAT TO DO BETWEEN WORKSHOPS

We ask if anyone would like to make any comments and, once the comments have come to an end, we suggest that during the following week we practice both conscious breathing and being assertive.

HOW DID THE ACTIVITIES GO?

Maybe they went really well, and you are happy with how they went.

Or maybe you didn't find it so easy. If that was the case, don't be discouraged! These things can take time. And of course, a lot depends on the ages of your children. And your own emotional situation. So just focus on the fact that practicing Skill 5 will be of enormous benefit for you and your children, now and in the future, and find a way that works for you to put it into practice.

In order to keep Skills 1, 2, 3, 4 and 5 in mind, do the conscious breathing activity regularly and incorporate visualizations of the five skills into the text.

QUESTIONNAIRE SKILL 5

KEY:
4-Totally Agree
3-Agree
2-Disagree
1-Totally Disagree

NOTE: Put a circle around the number of your reply.

a. Now I am aware of how to communicate better (by being assertive instead of aggressive or passive, i.e., taking into account my wishes but also those of others).
1— 2 — 3 — 4

b. Now I see how I can have better relationships with others and achieve my goals more easily (by being assertive).
1— 2 — 3 — 4

c. Now I can see that being assertive helps me find win-win solutions (instead of win-lose or lose-win) when there are problems or conflicts with others.
   1— 2 — 3 — 4
d. I would recommend this skill to my friends.
   1— 2 — 3 — 4

SKILL 6

LIVING CONSCIOUSLY
Having a Profound Sense of Serenity Almost Regardless of the Circumstances

By practicing this skill, we will be more aware of ourselves and others and be better able to calm ourselves when things happen that we don't like. When problems arise, as they inevitably will, we will be able to discuss them and resolve them. As a result, it is much less likely that anyone will store up grudges that may lead to estrangement.

Living consciously

Much of the time we are not aware of ourselves or of those around us. We often live on "automatic pilot."

In Skill 6, we learn how to feel calmer and more peaceful through breathing consciously, and how to be more aware of ourselves so that our automatic unconscious thinking does not rule our lives.

Conscious breathing

A large number of studies confirm the benefits of conscious, or mindful, breathing. Once learned, it can be practiced anywhere and at any time, to calm down, to feel good or to gain strength and energy.

Susan Kaiser, in her book *The Mindful Child*, said that bringing the practice of mindfulness to children and adolescents could profoundly change the world.

Benefits of conscious breathing:

- Reduces stress and blood pressure
- Prevents depression and anxiety
- Reduces the likelihood of burnout syndrome
- Increases motivation

- Improves academic performance
- Improves self-esteem
- Improves interpersonal relationships
- Reduces aggressiveness and violence

We can start by breathing consciously for a minute and, little by little, we can increase the time we devote to it. It is best to set aside a regular time every day when you will not be disturbed to do it together with your children. Once we have made a habit of breathing consciously, we can focus our attention on our breathing at any time and feel at peace.

Visualizing a difficult situation and changing how you feel about it

Incorporating visualizations into conscious breathing can be very beneficial. For example, you can visualize a situation about which you feel uncomfortable and reduce its impact on you by changing the way you look at the situation during the visualization.

In order to try this, think first of a situation in which you felt mildly uncomfortable.

Imagine the scene. Remember what happened, what you saw, what you thought, what you felt. Make the scene more intense — the colors more vivid, the sounds more immediate, your feelings stronger.

Now, in your imagination, see that scene as you were not part of it! Imagine that the scene has nothing to do with you personally.

Now turn down the colors. Make th[illegible] duller. Then make the scene black and white. Mak[illegible]o farther and farther away, see it get smaller and smaller. See it a long way in the distance.

And notice how your feelings become less intense.

Another way to do this is to make the scene smaller and smaller and then put it in a parcel and imagine yourself taking the parcel to the post office and sending it off to some far-off place!

You will find that the more you practice visualization, the less difficult situations will affect you.

Next, as you practice more, you can go on to apply visualizations to more difficult situations in which you have stronger feelings.

Example:
You find someone unfriendly. Now, while breathing consciously with your eyes shut, visualize yourself coming across that person and greeting them in a friendly way. Imagine them smiling and saying something friendly back. Do not be surprised if the next time you see them, they appear more friendly and even return your greeting in a friendly way!

Using visualization to change feelings about past events

Using visualization to help us give up an unhelpful thought or belief and establish a helpful new one can be very effective. The more you practice, the more effective it will be.

1. Sit down in a comfortable position, relax and close your eyes. Think of a mildly difficult situation in which you had uncomfortable feelings. Later you can choose more difficult situations to work with. Remember what

happened and how you felt. Ask yourself what you were thinking and whether your thoughts were helpful to you. If not, think of an alternative way you could have thought that would have caused you to feel less uncomfortable.

2. Imagine the situation. Remember what happened, what you saw, what you thought, what you felt.
3. Now continue to imagine the situation but this time think about it with your new COOL thought or belief.
4. Notice how differently you feel. Stay with your new thought and your new feeling for a minute or two.
5. Take a deep breath and open your eyes.

At first, do this sitting down, but later with practice you can do it in any situation and without closing your eyes.

Using visualization and imagination to prepare for future events

1. Sit down in a comfortable position, relax and close your eyes. At first you can do this in a special place you have chosen, and then, after you have practiced for some time, you will be able to do it anywhere.

   You are going to meet a group of friends. You don't drink alcohol, but you feel pressure to drink because your friends always offer you a glass. You feel like the odd person out for not doing what they do, and you want to prepare yourself to be able to say no.
2. Decide what kind of thoughts (Skill 1) will help you deal with this situation. Make sure that you are totally convinced by them and that they enable you to feel calm and relaxed.

3. Imagine the scene vividly. You are with your friends and, unlike them, you are drinking something nonalcoholic. Keep in mind the thinking you have decided on and monitor the way you are feeling. Now imagine that one of your friends offers you a glass of wine and that you say "no thanks" quite easily.
4. When you are ready, take a deep breath and open your eyes.
5. You can practice this by doing a role-play with another person.
6. Then try it out in real life! Have your helpful thought written down on a piece of paper, which you keep nearby. As one of your friends offers you a glass of wine, keep your helpful thought in mind and monitor the way you are feeling. Notice how good you feel when you say, "No thanks, I'm fine with this."

   Do this several times — the more you practice, the more you will become a master of the situation.

Practicing COOL thinking in difficult situations

Albert Ellis, the creator of REBT (see Skill 1), recommended seeking out a situation in which the very thing you don't like will be likely to happen and, when it happens, practicing your new COOL thinking and proving to yourself that you can manage your feelings even if circumstances are not to your liking.

For example, if you hate being criticized:

First, challenge your belief that you can't stand being criticized and choose a new COOL thought that totally convinces you. For example, "I don't like being criticized, but there is no law that exempts me from criticism and, if it happens, it is not the end of the world and I can stand it."

Next, imagine a situation in which you are being criticized and hold this new helpful thought in your mind so that being criticized has less effect, or no effect, on you.

Then seek out a situation in which you are likely to be criticized. Write your COOL thought on a postcard and have it by you. Keep this thought in mind while you listen to the criticism, and monitor how you are feeling. Afterward review how it went in order to improve the next time.

You can take action in this way in order to practice overcoming a large variety of situations, whether they are situations in which you feel criticized, ashamed, hurt or ignored. The more we practice, the more effective we will be in establishing new helpful ways of thinking and the less we will be affected by other people's comments and actions.

> "I am now more aware of my actions, my attitude.
> I remember saying that I was angry, but no,
> I can be more balanced in my emotions."
>
> **Parent**
>
> *From video at the end of Cool is Best workshops*

Our inner witness

Our witness is that part of ourselves that is able to observe ourselves, with our thoughts, beliefs, feelings and behaviors, nonjudgmentally from outside of ourselves.

This is not something we are used to doing and it might sound strange and perhaps impossible, but it is not difficult, and it is extremely beneficial. Observing ourselves enables us to see ourselves as we really are, or as others might see us if they could see us with all our thoughts and feelings.

When we see ourselves as we are, we see how much we judge, how many prejudices we have, and how often we are unjust and critical. As a result, we become humbler, more forgiving, and readier to see our faults. We judge and criticize less, and see others with more kindness, understanding and compassion.

Let's imagine that you have just finished an assignment and that you are pleased that you did it in spite of obstacles and distractions. Now see if you can see yourself from outside of yourself, and see yourself thinking that you are pleased and feeling great. Do it without judgment, without saying to yourself that it's good or bad.

Practice this and you will become more aware of whether you are thinking and chattering to yourself unhelpfully, and therefore having unnecessary unpleasant feelings and maybe acting in self-defeating ways. You may see yourself making excuses, self-justifying, criticizing, or you may see yourself thinking helpfully, feeling good and making good decisions. You will get to see how you are handling your life and you will become better able to see which unhelpful thoughts to challenge and change, and what you would do well to change in your life.

Some Eastern traditions teach that we have two identities. One of them is the real "I," the real "I" that is eternal and lives beyond our physical death. The other "I" is the personality that we have constructed with our thoughts and beliefs, feelings and experiences over the course of our lives. The "I" of the personality is the "mask" that we project to the world and that we have created in order to cope better with our challenges without having to look too deeply into who we are.

The witness is our real "I," our never-changing essence that is immortal, and the task that we face in life is to make our real "I" the principal actor in our lives instead of the "I" of personality.

The "I" of personality judges, demands, jumps to conclusions and journeys through life on an emotional roller coaster, whereas our real "I" sees and accepts things as they really are, without judgment and without attachment or demandingness or expectation, and it exists in a state of serenity and grace in which there is joy and an absence of suffering.

A meditation

There is a wonderful meditation of the monks of Ramakrishna that goes like this:

Imagine a great tree. This tree has a huge trunk and thousands of branches and millions of twigs and leaves. In this tree are two birds. One is perched high up at the top, still, serene and radiant. This bird is the real "I" and it is observing everything around it. Meanwhile, another bird is flitting about lower down the tree from branch to branch and from fruit to fruit. This second bird is the "I" of our personality and it gradually flits higher and higher up the tree until it eventually becomes quiet and merges with and becomes one with the bird at the top of the tree.

This meditation enables us to feel a sense of our true self and gives us a great sense of homecoming and peace. We can practice the meditation whenever we wish in order to feel serene and happy.

When we see ourselves with our witness, we see the world in a new way. We are not attached to anything, we do not depend on anything, we do not demand anything, and therefore nothing outside of ourselves has power over us. We watch our thoughts and our desires as they come and go, and we notice that things that were once of importance to us, and which delighted or disturbed us, are no longer of importance, and we see how nothing in life is permanent and how everything passes. We find we can, as a result, stop trying to change things and instead let go and accept things as they are.

Meditating in this way is not something esoteric that we have to do under the guidance of a guru. It is simply a way of allowing ourselves to have a quiet mind and be in touch with our inner self.

Having a mantram, or mantra

A mantram is a special word or sound that we choose, or that is given to us, that has no meaning and that we say to ourselves silently as we breathe consciously.

First, choose the word or sound. It can be anything that has no meaning in itself, such as "ohhum" or "shoorum." It can be whatever you feel good with. Now breathe consciously, and when you feel calm and connected, silently say the word you have chosen and repeat it in your mind as you breathe in and out. Later on, with practice, you will find that saying the mantram to yourself will bring you peace wherever you are. When difficult situations occur, you can say your mantram to yourself and you will feel the way you feel when you do conscious breathing.

Having time to be alone with oneself

If we want to get to know ourselves, we would do well to get into the habit of spending time alone for at least a few minutes a day. Many of us will do anything to avoid being alone, but if we try it and practice it and make it a habit, spending some time in solitude becomes a rich and essential part of our lives to which we look forward.

Zoltan Music, a contemporary painter and a survivor of the Nazi concentration camps, said that it was vitally important to him to spend time alone with himself — and by alone he meant being without any of the usual distractions we seek.

Henry David Thoreau withdrew from what he considered to be the hustle and bustle of life in 1845 and went to live at Walden Pond for two years in order to connect with himself and with nature. While he was there, he discovered many great truths, among them:

> "A man is rich in proportion to the number of things he can let alone."
>
> **Henry David Thoreau**
>
> *Walden*

Demandingness and attachment

We saw in chapter 1 that demandingness in our thinking and beliefs leads to strongly unpleasant emotions when things do not go the way we demand. This insight originally came from Buddha, one of whose teachings was that "attachment" is one of the principal causes of human suffering. By attachment he meant our being dependent on having a particular outcome or having things such as possessions in order to be happy.

Albert Ellis translated this insight into a form that we can practice in the modern era. Whereas Buddhism emphasizes living without attachment, Albert Ellis shows us how to live without being demanding, and thinking instead with preferences (see Skill 1).

This does not mean that we cannot desire and hope for things. We can of course desire and we can hope, but, if we *demand* and are therefore attached to things turning out the way we desire and hope, we should know that it will lead to our being unhappy.

If we think deeply about this and incorporate non-demandingness into our lives, we will be amazed at the difference it will make in a very short time to the way we feel about almost everything.

Our resistance to looking at ourselves

Knowledge about how to master our minds has been known since ancient days. Most human beings have not been much interested in it, yet there have always been some people who have sought to understand and transform themselves, and today there are many more people who are interested in doing so. To do this we do not need a guru!

> "You do not have to go to the mountain to meditate, rather bring the mountain to you."

Letting things go: Two monks and a woman at a river crossing

Long ago, two monks arrived at a great river on their way to visit a monastery. Also at the river bank was a woman waiting for the boatman in order to cross. As it turned out, there was no boatman at the crossing, and the only way to cross was to wade through the deep water.

The two monks were about to enter the water when one of them realized that the woman would be unable to do so on her own as the river was not only deep but also fast flowing. When the monk realized this, he offered to help her and carried her on his back to the other side. Once there, the two monks went on their way.

Several hours later, the second monk broke their silence and asked the first monk if he was not ashamed to have broken his vows to never touch a woman.

"No," said the first monk, "have you carried that thought with you all this way?"

ACTIVITIES TO DO TOGETHER WITH YOUR CHILDREN

PARENTS GUIDE: SKILL 6

LIVING CONSCIOUSLY

INTRODUCTION

These activities should be adapted to the ages of the children participating and to your own parental circumstances.

If you find the Six Skills of value, you can download the Cool is Best app, where you will find additional resources, including videos, audios, and interactive e-books for children from 8 to 14 years old.

Note for teachers: these activities are used successfully in Cool is Best workshops with students in school

INDEX (40 MINS)

1. Objectives, usefulness, materials
2. Brief review of previous workshops (5 mins)
3. Activity (20 mins) and group photo
4. Conscious breathing (5 mins)
5. Reflections (5 mins)
6. What have we learned today? The usefulness of the skill (5 mins)
7. What to do once the activities have finished

1a. OBJECTIVES

- Realizing that mindful breathing helps me to be more present.
- Realizing that mindful breathing helps me to feel calm, or to calm down if I am upset.
- Being aware of myself and my surroundings.
- Understanding how to use visualizations

1b. USEFULNESS OF THE SKILL

Conscious breathing helps me:

- Be aware of myself, of others and of my surroundings.
- To see myself as I am.
- Calm myself down.
- See things as they are rather than through a filter of prejudices.
- Face problems and make changes by means of visualizations.

1c. MATERIALS

- A4 white sheets
- Large sheets of paper (wallpaper type), white or colored
- Thick, colored markers for writing words for the group photo
- Small ball

2. REVIEW OF PREVIOUS SKILLS

We pass the ball, and the person who has the ball speaks if they wish.

Skill 1 – Managing my emotions by thinking COOL
Understanding that the way we think influences our emotions and our actions.

- Have we been aware of our HOT and COOL thoughts?
- How does thinking HOT make me feel? Does it make me feel worse? How does it affect me personally?
- If I think COOL, is it more likely that I will have better relationships with others?
- Can we give examples of when we have changed our thoughts from HOT to COOL and felt better?

Skill 2 – Recognizing my emotions
Being more aware of our emotions and how that helps us.

- Does it help us to name and talk about our emotions?
- Does that help others understand how we feel?

Skill 3 – Healthy self-esteem
Accepting ourselves and feeling good.

- What is the effect of HOT and COOL thoughts on our self-esteem?
- Is accepting myself as I am a COOL way of thinking?
- Does my self-esteem depend on my achievements, on having friends, on having a good job?
- If it does, what happens to my self-esteem if I no longer have these things?

Skill 4 – Listening with empathy
Helping others by listening with empathy.

- Have we been listening with empathy?
- Does listening with empathy improve our relationships? Can we give examples?

Skill 5 – Assertive communication
Taking into account the importance of our feelings and desires and those of others when we communicate.

- Does being assertive help us resolve conflicts on a win-win basis?
- Have we been more assertive? Can we give examples?

At the end, we can ask:

- Which of the skills, if any, helps us the most? Why?
- Have we started to apply some of what we have learned in our lives?
- Have the skills improved our relationships in the family?

3. ACTIVITY

We take some paper and draw, individually or together, a picture about something that we have enjoyed or have found helpful during the activities, and we put the drawings up on the wall.

PHOTO

Before ending the activity distribute sheets of A4 paper, folded in half, so that each person can write a word, large and in color, that represents what they have most enjoyed or benefitted from during the activities of all the Six Skills (for example: PEACE, EMPATHY, etc.).

Everybody also writes their reasons for choosing their word on the reverse side of their paper and, if they wish, shares the reasons with the others.

When everyone has written their word, and shared their reasons, someone takes a group photo of everyone holding their word in front of them.

4. CONSCIOUS BREATHING

If you have downloaded the Cool is Best app, you will find an audio recording for Skill 6 that you can also listen to if you wish.

Let's sit in a comfortable position with our eyes closed, our backs straight, our shoulders back in an open position and our feet in contact with the ground, without crossing our legs.

We put one hand on our stomach and the other on our chest and we notice that our body is moving, and that it is moving because of our breathing.

We have nothing else to do right now, we just focus our attention on our breathing. We focus our attention on the here and now, in the present moment.

We continue to breathe, each of us at our own pace. We focus our attention on our breathing. If any thought or concern arises, it doesn't matter. When we become aware of it, we simply turn our attention back to our breathing. If we like, we can transform the thought into a bird and let it fly away.

Now, while we continue to breathe, we also put our attention on our feet and on their contact with the ground.

We are going to feel very relaxed and heavy. This sensation goes up our legs, our knees. Our legs feel very relaxed and heavy. This sensation rises up our body, the lower part of the back and the stomach. We feel all these areas very relaxed, and we feel the pleasant sensation that relaxation gives us.

This sensation goes up the chest, the back, the shoulders. It goes down the arms and reaches the hands, which become very relaxed and heavy. It goes up the neck, the head, and reaches the eyes, the eyelids and the lips. We feel our whole body very relaxed and heavy. We continue to breathe, and we feel like our whole body is breathing.

Brief pause.

Now let's see ourselves from outside of ourselves as if we were someone else observing us. How do we see ourselves? Can we see ourselves from outside of ourselves? How are we feeling? Can we feel better when we choose to think COOL thoughts? Can we help others by listening to them with empathy? Can we be assertive and take into account both what we want and what others want, and find ways to resolve problems more easily?

Brief pause.

We continue to breathe, paying attention to our breathing. We take a deep breath, calmly and without exaggeration. A second breath. And a third. And little by little we move our toes, our bodies, our fingers, and we open our eyes.

After pausing a moment, we can talk about how the conscious breathing went. How did we feel? What did we notice?

Have we practiced during the week? We can recommend finding a time of day during the week (it is better if it is always the same time) to practice.

If some of us have difficulties, we can talk about them and remind ourselves that conscious breathing, like any skill, gets easier with practice.

> Those with whom we have problems are our most important teachers.

5/6. REFLECTIONS, WHAT DID WE LEARN TODAY, THE USEFULNESS OF THE SKILL

We have worked on this skill by practicing conscious breathing in all the previous five sessions.

- Do you think conscious breathing is helpful and, if so, why?

7. WHAT TO DO ONCE THE ACTIVITIES HAVE FINISHED

It is very beneficial to make a habit of applying the Six Skills to daily life: making sure that we are thinking COOL, being aware of our emotions, valuing ourselves, listening to others with empathy, communicating assertively, being aware of ourselves and our surroundings and doing mindful breathing for a few minutes every day, possibly incorporating visualizations such as the one that follows.

THE TWO BIRDS

We will start by closing our eyes and taking a few deep breaths. We breathe in through our nose and out through our mouth. We imagine that we are at the cinema in front of the screen where a movie is about to appear. As we continue to breathe, we see a green forest appearing on the screen. It is a forest that is full of trees. Little by little, we get closer to one of the trees. What is the tree like? Is it a big tree? A little one? What are its branches, its trunk and its roots like? Does it have many branches? Few branches? A lot of leaves? Few leaves? While we are imagining this tree, we see that there is a little bird on one of the branches.

Let's focus on the little bird. That little bird is very lively, and it hops from one branch to another, eating fruit as it goes. It does not stop moving about. It goes up, up, very high. And when it reaches the top, it meets another bird. That second bird is calm. It is a quiet bird that is observing everything rather than hopping about. It observes the meadows, the forest, the river, and the mountains in the distance.

When the first bird meets the quiet bird, it relaxes and stops hopping about. From here on, the two birds just observe quietly. The two birds are like the two parts of ourselves: the part that moves around searching, rarely satisfied, and the part of us that is quiet. These two little birds observe everything that happens around them from the top of the tree.

Now we take a few more breaths, paying attention to our breathing. We breathe in and we breathe out.

Let's take two more breaths. And one last one.

Now, little by little, we move our toes, our hands, our body, and we slowly open our eyes.

At the end of the visualization, put out some large sheets of paper and everyone, together or individually, draws the tree and the two little birds.

REFLECTIONS

Once everyone has finished drawing, you can ask:

- What do we think each bird represents?
- Did you notice that the active bird calmed down when it reached the bird at the top?
- What happens when we are not calm, but nervous? Can we think straight? Can we achieve what we want to achieve? Can we have good relations with others?
- How different is it if we are calm and at peace, like the bird at the top of the tree?

Teacher: "What happens when we are not calm?"
Students (10-year-olds): "We get restless… angry… nervous."
Teacher: "So now let's learn how to calm ourselves by breathing in a special way."

From video at the end of Cool is Best workshops

HOW DID THE ACTIVITIES GO?

Maybe they went really well, and you are happy with how they went.

Or maybe you didn't find it so easy. If that was the case, don't be discouraged! These things can take time. And, of course, a lot depends on the ages of your children and your own emotional situation. So just focus on the fact that practicing the skills will be of enormous benefit for you and your children, now and in the future, and find a way that works for you to put them into practice.

In order to keep the skills in mind and keep working

on them, you can do the conscious breathing activity regularly and incorporate visualizations of the Six Skills into the text. You can also create activities to do together yourself.

QUESTIONNAIRE SKILL 6

KEY:
4-Totally Agree
3-Agree
2-Disagree
1-Totally Disagree

NOTE: Put a circle around the number of your reply.

a. Now I am aware of how I can be calmer, especially in a difficult situation, by paying attention to my breathing and breathing more consciously.
1— 2 — 3 — 4

b. Now I see that I can benefit from visualizing difficult situations while breathing consciously.
1— 2 — 3 — 4

c. Now I see that I can become more aware of myself and everything around me.
1— 2 — 3 — 4

d. I would recommend this skill to my friends.
1— 2 — 3 — 4

e. The Six Skills have made an important positive contribution to my life and the life of my family.
1— 2 — 3 — 4

f. I believe that if we practice the Six Skills, it will be less likely that anyone in my family will cut off contact.
1— 2 — 3 — 4

EPILOGUE

The Six Skills are extremely helpful to us when painful events occur in our lives, but in order for them to be effective, we need to practice them; we often have deeply rooted counterproductive patterns of thought and behavior, and we need to create new habits.

A good way to do this at first is to practice on things that are not so important. For example, when we spill something on the floor, instead of getting upset, we can choose to think, "Well, it's not such a big deal, I'll clear it up in a second."

Then, you can respond to the fact that someone you know has maybe said something inconsiderate to you and, instead of saying to yourself, "What an unpleasant person she is, I always knew it!" you now say to yourself, "I don't like what she said, but maybe she's having a bad day and it's nothing to get upset about."

You can also practice with a friend by taking turns talking about your feelings and feeling the relief that comes from expressing them. When your friend talks about her feelings, you can practice listening with empathy, that is, listening actively, and you can ask for her feedback on whether the way you listened helped her so that you can improve. This is an invaluable skill when you have a problem with someone. Avoid trying to listen with empathy by email, because misunderstandings can easily occur.

It is also necessary to practice communicating assertively because it is vital for being able to reach win-win solutions with others. The key is to take into account other people's feelings and desires as well as your own, and to listen to them with empathy. This will encourage them to talk, which will enable you to learn more about the problem from their point of view, and make you better able to suggest solutions that may be acceptable to them.

By putting the Six Skills into practice in our daily lives, we will improve our mental health, have better relationships and a greater sense of well-being.

Now, as we turn the Six Skills into a habit, we are also training ourselves in case the day should come when we have the opportunity to reconnect with a person from whom we have estranged or become estranged. Should that happen, we will be thinking COOL, ready to listen with empathy, and ready to communicate assertively, taking into account that person's feelings and wishes as much as our own. We will prepare for the meeting by breathing consciously, feeling calm, and visualizing the meeting going well. Any problems that arise won't feel like the end of the world and we will be able to see the situation in perspective and deal with it better, even if the other person is unwilling to change.

You may remember the examples of Clara and Janna in the Introduction to the book. Well, Clara's children learned about the Six Skills and changed their thinking and Clara is now able to spend time happily with her grandchildren. Meanwhile, Janna eventually contacted her parents to ask them for their help when she realized that she needed to study for the exams that she had abandoned. Her parents suggested meeting their daughter together with a mediator. They had prepared themselves with the Six Skills over time and were able to listen to Janna actively with empathy. As a result, Janna felt reassured and an agreement was reached whereby her parents would support her studies — and this led, eventually, to further meetings and a restoration of their relationship and her finding a new partner.

NOTES AND REFERENCES

INTRODUCTION

1. Pillemer, Karl. 2020, *Fault Lines: Fractured Families and How to Mend Them*, Avery Publishing.
According to this book, family estrangement impacts over 100 million parents, siblings and other family members (both those estranging and those estranged) in the U.S., and affects all social classes, races and regions equally.
2. According to the charity *Stand Alone*, 12 million people are affected by family estrangement in the U.K.
3. Peele, Stanton. 2004, *7 Tools to Beat Addiction* and 2007, *Addiction-Proof Your Child*. Three Rivers Press.
4. Goleman, Daniel. 1995, *Emotional Intelligence*, Bantam Books.
5. Coleman, Joshua. 2021, *Rules of Estrangement*, Harmony Books.
6. Maté, Gabor, with Maté, Daniel. 2022, *The Myth of Normal*, Avery Publishing.
7. Palmer, Christopher. 2022, *Brain Energy*, BenBella Books.
8. The Stopbullying.gov website confirms that SEL helps prevent bullying.
9. **Benefits of the COOL IS BEST program for parents and teachers**
A group of more than 1,000 teachers and parents completed the COOL IS BEST online training program (with zoom follow ups) in 2021 and went on to teach the Six Skills to more than 100,000 children and students aged 5 to 18 years in 2021-2023. Over 90% of the group said:
"*Cool is Best helps me a lot to manage my emotions (Skill 1), recognize and express my emotions (Skill 2), accept and value myself and feel good about myself (Skill 3), listen with empathy to others who*

have problems (Skill 4), communicate assertively rather than aggressively or passively, and resolve problems on a win-win basis (Skill 5), be more aware of myself and others, and to be calmer (Skill 6)."

10. **Benefits of the COOL IS BEST program for children**

Over 90% of the group confirmed that:

"COOL IS BEST will help my children to manage their emotions better, create a better environment at home, respect others, study better, not be absent from school, not be violent and not take drugs."

A typical comment by teachers of kindergarten children who adapt the program to the ages of their students:

"I teach children ages 4 and 5 and have adapted the skills to their ages. The skills help the children to integrate in the group with the other children and flourish."

11. **Survey of teachers and parents (August 2023)**

SURVEY QUESTIONS	**ANSWERS Yes**
1-Have COOL IS BEST and the 6 Skills helped you?	92%
2-Have COOL IS BEST and the 6 Skills helped your students?	80%
3-Would many problems in the world be prevented or resolved if COOL IS BEST and the 6 Skills were practiced by all parents, teachers and children?	94%
4-Would you recommend COOL IS BEST to friends, family and colleagues?	94%

5-How many stars would you give COOL IS BEST? 5 STARS 4 STARS Average	 82% 16% 4.8/5
6-How many students have you taught the Six Skills to during 2021-2023? Average per teacher Total number of students when including teachers from other groups	 55 100,000 +

SKILL 1 – Managing our Emotions

The importance of being able to manage our emotions

Children who are able to control their emotions and their behavior are likely to do better both at home and at school and lead happier and more successful lives than children who do not do so. They are less likely to experiment with alcohol and drugs or develop problematical behaviors such as eating disorders or anti-social behavior. Moreover, when they become adults, they are likely to have fewer of the emotional problems that make many people's lives so difficult, and they are also likely to have better jobs and earn better salaries. The more that children are able to be in control of their feelings, the greater the sense they have of being in control of their lives, and the greater their self-belief, self-respect and self-esteem.

In contrast, children who do not have the ability to control their emotions are likely to cope badly with the ups and downs of life and will tend to be unhappier, give up more easily and, therefore, not do as well socially and academically.

1. There is an association in primary schools between self-regulation and academic success

Valiente, Carlos, Kathryn Lemery-Chalfant, Jodi Swanson, and Mark Reiser, 2008. "Prediction of Children's Academic Competence from Their Effortful Control, Relationships, and Classroom Participation." *Journal of Educational Psychology* 100 (1): 67–77.

2. There is an association between self-regulation and academic success in adolescents

Duckworth, Angela L. and Martin E P. Seligman, 2005. "Self-Discipline Outdoes IQ in Predicting Academic Performance of Adolescents." *Psychological Science* 16 (12): 939–944.

3. Self-regulation of emotions prevents the abuse of alcohol, delinquency and risky sexual behavior

It is essential that adolescents have the capacity to regulate their emotions because insufficient self-regulation of emotions is associated with the abuse of alcohol, drugs, delinquency and risky sexual behavior.

Quinn, Patrick D., and Kim Fromme, 2010. "Self-Regulation as a Protective Factor Against Risky Drinking and Sexual Behavior." *Psychology of Addictive Behaviors* 24 (3): 376–385.

4. The self-regulation of emotions prevents impulsiveness and self-harm in girls

For example, it prevents over-eating in order to assuage intense disagreeable emotions.

Stice, Eric, Katherine Presnell, and Diane Spangler, 2002. "Risk Factors for Binge Eating Onset in Adolescent Girls: A 2-Year Prospective Investigation." *Health Psychology* 21 (2): 131–138.

5. Being able to tolerate frustration and put off gratification is a defense against addiction

"The inability to delay gratification is an essential part of addiction."

Peele, Stanton, 2007. *Addiction-Proof Your Child.* p. 85, Three Rivers Press, New York.

6. The advantages of self-control

"Those who are better able to self-regulate demonstrate improved relationships, increased job success, and better mental health and are less at risk for developing alcohol abuse problems or engaging in risky sexual behavior."

Heatherton, Todd F, and Dylan D. Wagner, 2011. "Cognitive Neuroscience of Self-Regulation Failure." *Trends in Cognitive Science* 15 (3): 132–139. https://www.ncbi.nlm.nih.gov/pmc/articles/PMC3062191/.

7. How to be in control of one's emotions

Ellis, Albert, 2005. *How Rational Emotive Behavior Therapy Can Change Your Life Forever.* Amherst, NY. Prometheus Books.

SKILL 2 – Recognizing my emotions

The lack of emotion recognition predicts behavior problems

"We found that (low) self-esteem and (the lack of) emotion recognition, independently of each other, predicted behavioral problems."

Wells, Amy E. Laura M. Hunnikin, Daniel P. Ash, and Stephanie H. M. van Goozen, 2020. "Low Self-Esteem and Impairments in Emotion Recognition Predict Behavioral Problems in Children." *Journal of Psychopathology and Behavioral Assessment* 42 (1): 693–701. https://link.springer.com/article/10.1007/s10862-020-09814-7.

UCLA. "Putting Feelings Into Words Produces Therapeutic Effects In The Brain." *Science Daily*, 22 June 2007.

SKILL 3 – Having healthy self-esteem

1. The myth of self-esteem. The key importance of self-acceptance, acceptance of others, and acceptance of life itself.

Ellis, Albert, 2005. *How Rational Emotive Behavior Therapy Can Change your Life Forever.* Amherst, NY: Prometheus Books.

2. Low self-esteem predicts behavior problems.

"We found that (low) self-esteem and (the lack of) emotion recognition, independently of each other, predicted behavioral problems."

Wells, Amy E., Laura M. Hunnikin, Daniel P. Ash, and Stephanie H. M. van Goozen, 2020. "Low Self-Esteem and Impairments in Emotion Recognition Predict Behavioral Problems in Children." *Journal of Psychopathology and Behavioral Assessment* 42 (1): 693–701. https://link.springer.com/article/10.1007/s10862-020-09814-7.

3. There is an association between CBT and an increase in self-esteem.

"It appears that cognitive behavior play therapy group can help to effectively boost self-esteem and social skills of girls."

Siahkalroudi, Sareh Ghasemian, and M. Bahri, 2015. "Effectiveness of Cognitive Behavioral Play Therapy Group on Self-Esteem and Social Skills in Girls' Elementary School." *Health Psychology*.

4. The importance of parents giving unconditional positive regard (UPR), instead of conditional regard (CR), to their children.

"Parental styles characterized by UPR promote healthier adults (psychologically speaking) than parental styles characterized by CR."

Lopes, Daniela Rocha, Kees van Putten, and Peter Paul Moorman, 2015. "The Impact of Parental Styles on the Development of Psychological Complaints." *Europe's Journal of Psychology* 11 (1): 155–168. https://www.ncbi.nlm.nih.gov/pmc/articles/PMC4873100/.

5. Family environment and self-esteem development

"The present research improves our understanding of the link between family environment and children's self-esteem. Overall, the pattern of findings suggests that parental warmth, parental monitoring (knowing how and what children are doing and being interested, without being intrusive), low maternal depression, economic security, and presence of father positively predict child self-esteem, and that these effects hold across children's gender and age.... The findings suggest that effective interventions aimed at improving the self-esteem of children and adolescents should target relevant factors of the family environment. Improving the family environment might be particularly beneficial because research suggests that some of its effects on self-esteem might be enduring and shape children's self-esteem even when these children have grown up and become adults."

Krauss, Samantha, Ulrich Orth, and Richard Robins, August 2020. "Family Environment and Self-Esteem Development. A Longitudinal Study from Age 10 to 16." *Journal of Personality and Social Psychology* 119 (2): 457–478. https://www.researchgate.net/publication/335110307_Family_Environment_and_Self-Esteem_Development_A_Longitudinal_Study_from_Age_10_to_16.

6. The vital importance of secure attachment

The seminal work on this subject is John Bowlby's *A Secure Base.* Bowlby, John. 1988. *A Secure Base*. Tavistock/Routledge.

7. The vital importance to the young child of emotional connection to its mother.

Tronick, Edward. 1975.*The Still Face* experiment.

8. Another important author: Alice Miller

Miller, Alice. 1991. *The Drama of Being a Child.* Virago.

SKILL 4 – Listening with empathy

1. Supportive listening

"Supportive listening requires that the support listener demonstrate emotional involvement and attunement while attending to, interpreting, and responding to the emotions of the support seeker — a complex and challenging task."

Jones, Susanne M., January 2011. "Supportive Listening." *International Journal of Listening.* 25 (1): 85–103.

2. Many of us think that we are good listeners. But studies show that the average person only listens with 25% effectiveness.

Husman, Richard C., James M. Lahiff, and John M. Penrose, 1988. *Business Communication: Strategies and Skills.* Chicago: Dryden Press.

3. Listening well is extraordinarily important to us and to others.

The findings of this study apply to all of our relationships at home, school and work.

"To a large degree, effective leadership is effective listening. A study of managers and employees of a large hospital system found that listening explained 40% of the (different levels of effectiveness) in leadership."

Kramer, R., 1997. "Leading by Listening: An Empirical Test of Carl Rogers's Theory of Human Relationship Using Interpersonal Assessments of Leaders by Followers." PhD diss., George Washington University.

4. Studies and books showing that it is vital to listen, to both adults and children.

Rogers, Carl R., 1995. *On Becoming a Person*, Houghton Mifflin.

Gordon, Thomas., 1970. *P.E.T. – Parent Effectiveness Training.* Plume, Penguin Group.

Axline,Virginia M., 1969. *Play Therapy*. Ballantine Books.

Axline, Virginia M., 1964. *Dibs in Search of Self; Personality Development in Play Therapy.* Ballantine Books.

Rosenberg, Marshall, B., 1999. *Nonviolent Communication.* Puddledancer Press.

Gottman, John. 2011. *Raising an Emotionally Intelligent Child: The Heart of Parenting.* Simon & Schuster.
Gottman reports that his own studies show (p. 68) that children who are listened to with empathy and thus helped to express and manage their emotions, do better in terms of academic achievement, health, peer relationships and behavior, and are better able to deal with distressing situations.

"More than IQ, your emotional awareness and ability to handle feelings will determine your success and happiness in all walks of life."

SKILL 5 – Communicating with assertiveness

"Taking into account how the other person feels … so that they feel heard … and (are) less likely to be defensive."

"Simple acts of initial language use can reduce the chances that conflict discussion will descend into a downward spiral of hostility …. Using I-language and communicating perspective were both found to reduce perceptions of hostility. For example: 'I understand you feel that way, but I feel this way.'"

Rogers, Shane L., Jill Howieson, and Casey Neame, 2018. "I Understand You Feel That Way, But I Feel This Way: The Benefits of I-Language and Communicating Perspective during Conflict." *Peer J.* 6 (e4831). https://www.ncbi.nlm.nih.gov/pmc/articles/PMC5961625/.

Holt, John. *How Children Fail*, 1964, and *How Children Learn*, 1967. Pitman Publishing Company.

John Holt became a leading voice for the home-educating movement in the 1960s and wrote a number of inspiring best-selling books about how children learn and how adults can help them most, including by not being authoritarian, providing them with a stimulating environment and letting them take charge of their own learning.

SKILL 6 – Living consciously

1. "Based on an examination of empirical literature across multiple methodologies, this review concludes that mindfulness and its cultivation facilitates adaptive psychological functioning."

Keng, Shian-Ling, Moria J. Smoski, and Clive J. Robins, 2011. "Effects of Mindfulness on Psychological Health: A Review of Empirical Studies." *Clinical Psychology Review.* 31 (6): 1041–1056.

2. Randomized control trial of effects of TM meditation
"Conclusions: This is the first RCT to demonstrate that a selected mind-body intervention, the TM program, decreased blood pressure in association with decreased psychological distress, and increased coping in young adults at risk for hypertension." This mind-body program may reduce the risk for future development of hypertension in young adults.

Nidich, Sanford I., Maxwell V. Rainforth, David A. F. Haaga, John Hagelin, John W. Salerno, Fred Travis, Melissa Tanner, Carolyn Gaylord-King, Sarina Grosswald, and Robert H. Schneider, 2009. "A Randomized Controlled Trial on Effects of the Transcendental Meditation™ Program on Blood Pressure, Psychological Distress, and Coping in Young Adults." *Am Jnl of Hypertension.* 22 (12): 1326–1331.

3. Two researchers at Kent State University have found that mindfulness-based stress reduction (MBSR) can reduce high blood pressure which affects nearly 60 million adults in the United States.
"MBSR, which involves the practice of meditation, body awareness and some gentle yoga, has been shown to be effective in preventing and treating depression and anxiety and alleviating stress, but scientific studies of its effects on blood pressure are rare."
Hughes, Joel W., and David M. Fresco, 2013. "Meditation Effective in Reducing Blood Pressure" Kent State University.

4. Mindful breathing in New York City schools

The mayor of New York City, Eric Adams, announced in June 2023 that mindful breathing will be required in NYC schools from 2024.

5. Some highly recommended books

Rinpoche, Akong Tulka, 1994. *Taming the Tiger.* Rider and Co.
Nhat Hanh, Thich, 1992. *Towards Inner Peace.* Plaza y Janés (Spanish edition).
Dalai Lama, 1996. *The Power of Compassion.* Thorsons.
Tolle, Eckhart, 2002. *Practicing The Power of Now.* New World Library.
Ajahn, Sumedho, 1992. *Citaviveka.* Amaravati Publications.
Easwaran, Eknath, 2008. *Mantram Handbook.* Nilgiri Press.
Herrigel, Eugen, 1953. *Zen in the Art of Archery.* Pantheon Books.
Mitchell, Stephen (trans), 1990. *Tao Te Ching.* Kyle Cathie
Nicholl, Maurice, 1996. *Psychological Commentaries on the Teachings of Gurdjieff.* Samuel Weiser.
Kabat-Zinn, Jon, 2009. *Wherever You Go, There You Are: Mindfulness Meditation in Everyday Life.* Hachette.
Kaiser Greenland, Susan, 2010. *The Mindful Child: How to Help Your Kid Manage Stress and Become Happier, Kinder, and More Compassionate.* Simon and Schuster.

INDEX

MORE FROM COOL IS BEST

App: "***Cool is Best: The 6 Skills***" The app for parents and children includes videos of CIB workshops, audios, and interactive e-books for children 8 to 12 years old. It can be downloaded on Google Play Store and Apple App Store. English and Spanish.

For information about the CIB app for teachers, which includes training videos and the complete program for students ages 8 to 14, please visit www.coolisbest.com.

App: ***My Emotions with Rani and Friends*** A fun and engaging way for young children from 4 to 8 years old to learn more about emotions. Charming characters and illustrations. English and Spanish. Google Playstore and Apple App Store.

App: ***Tree House*** More fun with Rani! Educational games and activities for children ages 4 and above. Charming characters and illustrations. English and Spanish. Google Playstore and Apple App Store.

Online Sessions To share experiences of implementing COOL IS BEST with others. Hosted by a CIB psychologist. To book go to coolisbest.com.

For links and more resources please visit www.coolisbest.com

NOTES

Made in the USA
Middletown, DE
01 July 2024

56630428R00144